# The 3 A's
## Align, Assign and Accomplish

*Christian Life and Development*

D. S. Reynolds
Poems by H. Henry

**Kingdom Publishers**

The 3 A's: Align, Assign and Accomplish
Christian Life and Development
Copyright© D. S. Reynolds

All rights reserved. No part of this book may be reproduced in any form by photocopying or any electronic or mechanical means, including information storage or retrieval systems, without permission in writing from both the copyright owner and the publisher of the book. The right of D. S. Reynolds to be identified as the author of this work has been asserted by her in accordance with the Copyright, Designs and Patents Act 1988 and any subsequent amendments thereto.
A catalogue record for this book is available from the British Library.

All Scripture Quotations have been taken from the New International Version, The Living Bible and the King James Version of the Bible.

ISBN: 978-1-913247-79-9

1st Edition by Kingdom Publishers
Kingdom Publishers
London, UK.

You can purchase copies of this book from any leading bookstore or email contact@kingdompublishers.co.uk

# Dedication

*I give all credit to God Almighty for the strength, motivation, wisdom and life experiences that He has given me to write this book. He is so loving, patient and kind. Thank God he does not give up on us! I also want to dedicate this book to my husband and two sons. If it wasn't for them much of this book would not have been written. Thanks guys! Finally thank you to my parents, siblings and church family. You know who you are and the encouragement you have given me whilst on this journey. I love you all.*

# Acknowledgement

I was inspired to write this book at the beginning of January 2019. As I was relaxing in my chair at home, the words, *Align, Assign and Accomplish,* came to me. I meditated on these words for a while and then began to make some very brief notes. I began to realise that aligning ourself with God and His Word enables us to excel to another dimension and that this, in turn, equips us to be assigned to designated tasks that He wants us to accomplish. This process takes the focus away from us and puts the emphasis on God, as we begin to recognise and accept that we are His vessels and He is the one who is working in and through us. Thus, enabling His will to be accomplished not only in our lives, but in the lives of others, as they too are impacted and touched by Him.

I then began to tell people that I was writing a book and told them the title. Their immediate response was, "Wow!" It was then that I realised this was something that I had to do. This was my assignment, and once I accepted it, everything else fell into place. A few days later a friend gave me a book to read that helped to motivate me put pen to paper. Other friends and family members also encouraged me. I am a relatively quiet person who prefers to work in the background and encourage others to pursue their goals, so to write a book is out of character for me, that is why I know this book has been an assignment from God.

I give all due credit to God Almighty for the strength, motivation, wisdom and life experiences He has given to me in order that I could write this book. I hope it will be an encouragement to others who are led to do something for God that may be out of character for them too.

It is only when we come out of our comfort zone and are challenged, that we can see who we really are and what we are able to achieve, as God empowers us to do His work. It is like a journey of discovery that can be extremely exciting but can also bring an element of fear. The important thing is to at least take the step and try. I could have allowed the words align, assign and accomplish to lie dormant, never put pen to paper and not know the outcome or impact this book may have on someone's life. That said, I decided to align myself with this assignment and regardless of the outcome, I have accomplished the task by the grace of God.

I am grateful to Hannah, a gifted poet and member of my church. Her wonderful contributions can be seen at the end of each chapter. Thank you sister Hannah.

I am also grateful for my friends who did not give up on me but persevered with their friendship towards me and made such a huge impact upon my life. They have helped me to become the person that I am today, and I am truly grateful. Thank you and I love you all.

Finally, I want to acknowledge my late brother, Pastor Franklin James, who was truly a man of God; able to teach and preach the inspired Word of God impacting my life and the life of so many people. His legacy continues today. Thank you, Pastor Franklin. We love you and miss you.

Unless otherwise mentioned, Bible quotes are taken from The Living Bible (TLB), copyright ©1971 by Tyndale House Foundation, Illinois.

*The names of the characters have been changed to protect the identity of the individuals.*

# Contents

| | |
|---|---|
| INTRODUCTION | 13 |
|     Masks | 18 |
| CHAPTER ONE | |
|     Letting Go! | 19 |
|     Why? | 30 |
| CHAPTER TWO | |
|     What is Alignment? | 31 |
|     You Can't Have Me! | 47 |
| CHAPTER THREE | |
|     What about the Assignment? | 48 |
|     The Cares of Life | 66 |
| CHAPTER FOUR | |
|     The Reality of Being Assigned | 67 |
|     Little Me.... | 88 |
| CHAPTER FIVE | |
|     Living in Alignment | 89 |
|     Do you Remember? | 100 |
| CHAPTER SIX | |
|     You Choose what You Accomplish | 101 |
|     Quiet | 114 |
| CHAPTER SEVEN | |
|     Little by Little, God will Give you what's Yours | 115 |
|     No Condemnation | 125 |

CHAPTER EIGHT
    What about our Assignment and Children?      126
    Identity      136

CHAPTER NINE
    The Outcome of the Assignment      137
    It Doesn't Matter      156

CHAPTER TEN
    Being Out and Coming Back into Alignment.      157
    No more Looking Back.      174

CHAPTER ELEVEN
    Putting the 3 A's Together.      175
    Broken Identity      185

PRAYER      186

REFERENCES      187

# Introduction

It was the summer school holidays - six weeks of consistent sunshine and bright skies. My younger sister and I made our house and garden a place of adventure, playing hide and seek, watching children's television, making dolls houses out of cardboard boxes, playing school and developing our creative skills. It was fun. We used our imagination extensively in those days and created our own entertainment. There was very little technology. Money was limited so there were no family holidays and in addition to this we had a large family.

I was understandably very excited when, during one such summer holiday, we went on a day trip to London with our parents to visit our paternal aunt. I was only around six or seven years old at the time. It was exciting travelling by car down the motorway and stopping off at the service station to eat our homemade sandwiches. After a few hours, we arrived in London and drove down a quiet side street where we were flanked by rows of terraced houses on both sides.

We finally stopped outside a Victorian terraced house with a small front yard. The house did not look particularly large from the outside, however, when we went inside, it was quite imposing. The house had at least three reception rooms and a small kitchen on the ground floor. My aunt lived in the house with her husband and she also accommodated a young family friend. He was a young man who looked to be in his early twenties.

When we entered the house, our aunt and uncle were very welcoming and prepared refreshments for us. As children, we were on our best behaviour as the unspoken rule was; *children were seen and not heard.* My sister and I kept our selves entertained by interacting with each other and watching the television.

When we were due to leave, my younger sister was given a doll by the family friend. I waited in anticipation for my doll too, but I did not receive one. Inside, I was devastated. Up until that point I did not see a difference between my siblings and myself. I never felt that I was treated differently by my siblings or my parents but at that moment, I asked myself why I did not get a doll and was there something wrong with me.

Looking back now, that was the moment when my self-doubt began to emerge and I began to question myself. I began to think that other people were better than I was. I found myself seeking approval and validation from others. I thought I could achieve this by *being nice* to everyone in order to be accepted and not rejected. This eventually became the norm as I grew older.

I know this sounds dramatic and extreme but that was the reality at the time. I did not think, perceive or comprehend that the family friend probably gave my sister the doll because she was the *baby of the family.* In all honesty, looking back now, he did not need to have a reason as that was his prerogative.

Many children at this stage of development are sensitive to external experiences and respond to them accordingly. *That's not fair* is a term often expressed by some young children who feel they have been treated unjustly even though they may not have been. They have their own perception of what is right and what is wrong. Others are not so expressive, for whatever reason, and so internalise what they are feeling. I was one of those children; I internalised my feelings.

I am sure my experience is not unique. What it does do, however, is to highlight that we all arrive in this world with our attributes, confidence, creativity, inquisitiveness, gifts and talents, and in one moment, all of that can be derailed.

Our parents, carers, families, the environment, society, the media, teachers and our own experiences impact upon us either positively or negatively and thus help to shape who we are and what we become.

The fullness of the impact is not realised until much later on in life. For example, some children grow up into adulthood with issues similar to what I experienced and, if not addressed, this can impact upon their decision-making processes later on in life. This impact can be the difference between living a life that is based on survival techniques or living a life that is fulfilled and abundant.

Life is not about surviving. To survive means to continue to live or exist, especially against the odds of danger or hardship. No! Life is about living to the full potential of what you were designed and created to become.

John 10:10 (KJV)

*The thief cometh not, but for to steal, and to kill, and to destroy: I am come that they might have life, and that they might have it more abundantly.*

John 10:10 (TLB)

*The thief's purpose is to steal, kill and destroy. My purpose is to give life in all its fullness.*

Jesus is saying the thief (Satan) who is the enemy of God has the ultimate plan to kill, steal and destroy our lives but Jesus has come to give us LIFE.

Life is about becoming who we are meant to be from God's perspective so that we can be fulfilled and impact the lives of those around us in a positive way. It is about recognising that we all have something to contribute in this world.

In order to do that it requires us to be aligned. We need to come in line with the God who designed and created us for His purposes.

We need to go beyond the perceptions of how we see our self, and beyond the preconceived ideas of how others perceive us; including our family, friends, husband, wife, colleagues, or whoever we allow to influence us. The difficulty with perception is that it is often based on interactions and personal interpretations, assumptions and judgments, which are not always correct and therefore, can be misleading. This can then influence the direction of our relationships and the direction of our life.

Sometimes we struggle to interpret and understand things that we have encountered in life. There are occasions when our interpretation of an encounter is later confirmed and is therefore, deemed to be correct. There may also be occasions where our interpretations are incorrect, thus leading us to draw the wrong conclusion.

It is at these times that we can become misaligned as we go off track due to a misunderstanding, inaccurate interpretation or simply not having all of the factual information. In such cases, we often need help to get back on track so that we can be realigned. In the case of the doll, I became misaligned due to my misinterpreting the situation, and as a result it has had a negative impact on my life.

To illustrate this point, I have to confess that I am terrible at directions. Prior to the introduction of satellite navigation systems, I struggled to read maps and, as a result, there were occasions when I would get lost. I would ring my husband at work and say, "I'm lost can you help me?"

The first thing he would ask is, "Where are you?" He needs to know my starting point in order to navigate me to my destination.

Once I have given him a landmark, he then consults a map and helps me get back on track. However, he first had to locate my position and then give me the directions.

I also trust him and know he is competent to give me the correct information as I have seen him plan his journey many times prior to taking a trip. Without his help, I would have been driving around aimlessly and frustrated. He has tried to pass his map reading skills on to me, but it is one of those things at which I have never really succeeded. I thank God for him and my SatNav.

My point is that sometimes life can feel like we are on a journey where we feel lost and frustrated. We may have misinterpreted something that lead us down the wrong road or we may even have been misled.

Sometimes, the questions need to be asked: Where am I? How did I get here? Have I taken a wrong turn? What help do I need to get back on track? Where am I going? Who can I trust to help me get back on track? These are all important questions and we may not have all the answers but none of them can be addressed until we are willing to acknowledge and admit we need to take a new direction.

Once an acknowledgement has been made, we can then seek the right assistance to help us move forward in the right direction without feeling like a failure, stuck or ashamed.

This book will take you on a journey

- from being out of position or stuck, to a place where you can come into the correct position. (Alignment)
- to enable you to comprehend and undertake and fulfil your Assignment
- to enable you to achieve what you were created to do and impact the lives of others. (Accomplish the task)

The challenge now is to be *ALIGNED, ASSIGNED AND ACCOMPLISH.*

# Masks

*Going along pretending all is fine, smiling,*
*greeting and waving goodbye.*
*Conversations held like all's alright.*
*Saying I love you, whilst numb inside.*

*Can anyone see the hidden truth...?*
*That pain deep down, it's like an aching tooth.*
*Going to the dentist to get an extraction,*
*Wouldn't take away this pain, no... it's not even a distraction.*
*So, who can help give me peace of mind?*

*When I've looked all over and tried to confide,*
*in things temporary, materialistic, even friends by my side.*
*With all their help...which is so very kind,*
*Only Jesus can hug me from the inside.*

**H. Henry**

# Chapter One

## Letting Go!

Fast forward; I am now sixteen years old. My parents are going through a divorce and life is turned upside down. With the unresolved issues of self-doubt and low self-esteem things appear to get worse not better. When my father left the marital home, I decided to get a Saturday job whilst I was still at school. I felt so insecure that I needed to have my own income, so I could *support* myself and gain some independence.

I continued to exude a façade that everything was okay and just got on with life. I was not particularly motivated at school and it is fair to say that the teachers did not have high expectations either. At the age of sixteen, I swayed between different career options. I thought about becoming a nurse as my mother had been a nurse. I then thought about being a secretary because my sister was a secretary. I then decided to go to sixth form college as I had to repeat many of my O-levels, as they were called back then. I had failed most of them at school. I spent the next three years completing O-levels and then A-Levels.

I had seriously considered becoming a child psychologist as I thoroughly enjoyed psychology as a subject. However, when I was told that there was a requirement that I had to teach in a school for two years, the thought of teaching and my own insecurities scared me so much I diverted away from that career. Then, one day my psychology teacher said, *"You would make a good social worker."* Do not underestimate the power of words. Those words were spoken into my life and as a consequence of not really knowing who I was and what I could achieve and what I wanted to do, I captured those words like a fisherman captures fish in a net.

After four years of university, I qualified as a social worker and remained in that field for almost seventeen years. I learned a great deal about people, relationships, children and families. It was not a negative experience and as my friend often says, *"Nothing is wasted."* In retrospect, this experience highlights what was discussed earlier regarding seeking to please others and valuing someone else's opinion above your own. This happens when we do not know who we really are, what we want, what we can achieve and what our gifts and talents are.

Instead of directing the course of our lives, we allow others to direct it for us. Subsequently, we later wonder why we sometimes become depressed, stressed, unhappy and unfulfilled whilst going through the motions of life. Those adjectives do not sound like an abundant life to me.

That said, it is also important to highlight that sometimes others may see a quality or a talent within you and make suggestions of what might be a suitable career path for you. As an individual, you still need to take ownership of what you want to achieve in life and not do something just to appease or please someone else. It is very hard to live somebody else's dream or ambition if you do not take ownership of it yourself because that too can lead to an unfulfilled life.

During the journey of my parent's divorce, I became a Christian. I observed other family members who had become Christians and I could see that there were positive changes that had taken place in their lives. I accepted Jesus Christ into my life and that was a defining moment in a positive way. I had been visiting a church occasionally and then my sister's friend invited her to attend a church convention. My sister did not want to attend by herself and so asked me to go with her and I ended up giving my life to Christ at that meeting. I repented of my sins, which means I turned away from the behaviours that caused offence to God. Whilst on that journey, I realised that we have all caused offence to God in some way or another.

Romans 3:23

> Yes, all have sinned; all fall short of God's glorious ideal;

An example of this can be seen in one of the ten commandments found in Exodus 20:16, You must not lie.

I remember when my eldest son, was around three years old, he decided to draw pictures on the wall, as some children do at that age. I approached him and asked him, *"Why have you drawn on the wall?"*

His response was, *"But you didn't see me, did you?"*

I was so shocked by his tone and response that I paused for a while in order to process what he had said. I then composed myself and said, *"Well, Mummy didn't do it and Daddy didn't do it, so it had to be you."*

He was right, I *had not* seen him, but the shock for me was his capacity to reason and not accept responsibility for what he had done, as he was not caught in the act.

It is amazing how children of a certain age know when they have done something wrong. However, their immediate response is to protect themselves and they lie, deny or blame someone else in order to avert blame. The question needs to be asked, who taught them to lie, deny or blame at such a young age. The fact is children are not taught. This type of behaviour is innate and when parents, carers or teachers observe such behaviour, they usually correct those responsible and inform them that it is *wrong*; just like I did with Alex.

It is unfortunate that despite being corrected, such behaviour can often continue well into adulthood.

Psalms 51:5–6

*But I was born a sinner, yes, from the moment my mother conceived me.*

*You deserve honesty from the heart; yes, utter sincerity and truthfulness. Oh, give me this wisdom.*

This verse reiterates that we are born with sin. Therefore, none of us are immune from causing offence to God regardless of how *good* we think we are. The concept of *good* is also relative and means different things to different people. That is why we ourselves, cannot determine the base line for *good*.

Luke 18:18-19

*Once a Jewish religious leader asked him this question, "Good sir, what shall I do to get to heaven?"*

*"Do you realise what you are saying when you call me 'good'?" Jesus asked him. Only God is truly good, and no one else.*

In light of this, I recognised that I was not a *good* person and was thankful that, when I became a Christian, I was forgiven for the offences I had caused to God in my life. I was then baptised by full immersion. This was my public statement that I had made the decision to follow Christ. It was also a representation of being born again. I received the gift of the Holy Spirit of God which empowers me to live a life in alignment with God's word. Without the Spirit of God, it would be impossible to achieve this.

John 14:15–17

*If you love me, obey me; and I will ask the Father and he will give you another Comforter, and he will never leave you. He is the Holy Spirit, the Spirit who leads into all truth. The world cannot receive him, for it isn't looking for him and doesn't recognize him. But you do, for he lives with you now and someday shall be in you….*

I began to study my Bible and pray as I really wanted to know more about God. I remember getting up in the early hours of the morning and seeking God in prayer; undertaking my Bible study before going to college. Whilst at college, I would read my Bible during my lunch times and breaks. No one told me to do this. The desire and motivation came from the Spirit of God that I had received after accepting Jesus Christ into my life.

Jeremiah 29:13 (KJV)

*And ye shall seek me, and find me, when ye shall search for me with all your heart.*

If you are hungry you seek food to satisfy your hunger. The same principle applies when you are *hungry* for God. If you seek Him, He will reveal Himself to you and satisfy that hunger.

Although I appeared to be happy on the outside, there were still unresolved issues that needed to be addressed on the inside including my feelings regarding my parents' divorce.

Just because you become a Christian, does not mean that everything becomes perfect immediately. You will still have challenges to deal with from the past, the present and in the future. The difference is how you deal with those challenges as a *born-again* Christian.

When you look at the life of Jesus Christ, He was often criticised for interacting with the rejects, undesirables and dysfunctional people in society. The pious people of the day could not comprehend why He wanted to mix with such individuals.

Matthew 9:10–13

> *Later, as Jesus and his disciples were eating dinner at Matthew's house, there were many notorious swindlers there as guests.*
>
> *The Pharisees were indignant. "Why does your teacher associate with men like that?"*
>
> *"Because people who are well don't need a doctor. It's the sick people who do." was Jesus' reply. Then he added, "Now go away and learn the meaning of this verse of Scripture, "It isn't your sacrifices and gifts I want - I want you to be merciful". For I have come to urge sinners, not the self-righteous back to God."*

Jesus was saying He had come for those who are broken, hurting, wounded, dysfunctional and generally all those who recognise that they are in need of Him. In my view that is all of us, because we have all experienced some kind of hurt, pain, rejection and or exposure to some form of dysfunctional relationship in life whether intentionally or unintentionally.

However, there are others who are self-righteous, who see themselves as *good* and are judgmental towards others. These are the people who think they do not need to be forgiven because according to their standards, they have not offended God and they are okay.

Individuals who hold such opinions are missing out on the wonderful blessings God wants to give them. They are not in a place to humbly receive such blessings because they have everything *sorted* in their lives and therefore, have no need of Him.

I am not ashamed to say that the impact of my parent's divorce affected me. I would also say, do not underestimate the impact of divorce on children. It is possible for a child to harbour bitterness towards a loved one as result of the words used by one parent to express their dissatisfaction with their former spouse. This can adversely impact a child and contribute to their misalignment later on in life. It could even impact upon their future relationships.

As I began to study the word of God, somehow bitterness and the Christian message of forgiveness and love your neighbour, seemed incompatible. Therefore, I knew I had problems. This is what the word of God does; it convicts you and helps you realise that something is not right in your life. It brings things to your attention that are out of alignment with the word of God. You choose how you respond to that conviction. Some people ignore it and continue to justify their behaviour. Others may acknowledge it but that is as far as it goes. Others may acknowledge it and maybe try to do something about it. The choice is ours, but we must also be prepared to accept the consequence of how we respond to our convictions.

My younger siblings had regular contact with our father, as they had more flexibility and were still at school. I was at college during the week, worked on Saturdays and went to church on Sundays. I remember one day my father brought one of my siblings home and asked to see me as I was at home on that particular occasion and he had not seen me for a while. I remember feeling anger and bitterness inside and my heart was beating quickly as I approached his car. He then leaned forward from the driver's seat and asked, *"Why do you hate me so much?"* I just looked at him and could not answer as it was true. As I was not encouraged to express my views as a child, there was no way I was going to express them now. *How could I answer that question; especially a question like that?* I remember just staring at him; a frozen glare in my eyes.

Some months later, I was standing at the counter of the retail store where I worked. It was a typical Saturday afternoon. I heard a voice inside saying, *You need to go and see your Dad.*

My immediate reaction was, *I can't, I don't know how to get to his house,* which was true as I seldom went to see him.

I knew God was speaking to my heart through the Holy Spirit because that was not a thought that I would have entertained or even suggested to myself. I tried to talk myself out of it but then I decided to accept the challenge.

One dark winter evening after work, I felt as though I was being ushered to the bus stop. I stepped on the correct bus and managed to find his house. When I knocked on his door, he was so shocked, he just stood there and called my name out loudly. I just stood there too; not knowing what was going to happen next. We both opened our arms and we hugged each other.

In that moment, I literally felt the bitterness, anger and anxiety leave and an overwhelming release of God's love flowed through my body. I no longer felt the anger, hatred or pain. I felt free and peaceful inside. I then went into his house and we began to talk and I knew that was the beginning of a broken relationship being healed.

Matthew 6:14–15

> *Your heavenly Father will forgive you if you forgive those who sin against you; but if you refuse to forgive them, he will not forgive you.*

Some people look at forgiveness as a weakness but actually, it is a strength. Forgiveness is a powerful *key* that releases you and enables you to come out of a place of negativity, and empowers you to release someone else from their negativity too. However, it is up to them whether they choose to remain in that place of negativity or to step out in freedom. The ultimate choice is theirs as we cannot control the response of others, but we can control our own response.

The word of God reinforces that we have a responsibility to try to live at peace with everyone, but it will not always be possible. If we apply the principle of at least trying, and this is not received, then at least we have tried, God will honour that. It is not for us to take revenge. We have to leave that person to God for Him to do whatever He needs to do in the life of that person.

Romans 12:18–19

> *Don't quarrel with anyone. Be at peace with everyone, just as much as possible.*
>
> *Dear friends, never avenge yourselves. Leave that to God, for he has said that he will repay those who deserve it. Don't take the law into your own hands.*

Exercising forgiveness enabled me to experience a feeling of freedom and not guilt. I remember going home later that evening and my mother asking me where I had been. She was used to me coming home straight after work. I told her that I went to visit my father and she very wisely made no comment.

On reflection, the reason why I had kept away from my father was because I did not appreciate how negatively he spoke about my mother at times. I also did not want to upset my mother or hurt her feelings although she never said that if I saw him, this would upset her. Assumptions can affect behaviour, which in turn affects the outcome of relationships.

A close friend of mine, a few years older than me, was married with young children. From my perspective, she was established in her life. I was around nineteen or twenty years old at the time. We became very good friends and I learnt so much from her. We used to talk about many different issues, and one day she asked me a question and I responded in my usual way, which was to agree with everything that she had said. She then said, *"What is wrong with you? You always agree with everything I say, and you never seem to have your own opinion."*

I was devastated. I assumed we had a great friendship, but from her perspective something was lacking. The comment she made was then always in the back of my mind. I was now conscious of something that I did not know how to resolve. There were times when I would reflect upon what she said, and once again feel guilty as I knew she was right, but I had no solution to the problem. Therefore, it became one of those issues that I filed away in the cabinet of my mind until the opportunity arose to address it.

At the age of twenty, I was offered a place at Sheffield Hallam University. This was a huge achievement for me considering my family background and experiences. I was so excited to be leaving home and embarking on my new life as a student in a new city; undertaking a degree and diploma. It was a new challenge and a completely new experience as I was the first one in my immediate family in the UK to go to university.

At the beginning of the course, all the students had to gather together for a meeting. I briefly introduced myself to some of the other students. I was still not very confident and as a result, I did not make the effort to develop any close friendships. Partly because of the investment it would take (I was not prepared to make it) and secondly, I did not want to get too close to anyone for fear of being rejected.

There was a young student on the same course who attempted to befriend me over the next few weeks and invited me to various social activities. I did not commit myself to attend any of the events and finally, one day in frustration, she said, *"What's wrong with you? I am only trying to be your friend and you seem to have brick walls around you."* Once again I realised I still had more issues. I later identified I had issues trusting people and not wanting to get too close in case I let them down or in case they let me down.

It was at that point that I realised I had some very deep issues that needed to be dealt with. I did not know how or what to expect during this process, but I knew it would involve me becoming vulnerable and I knew things had to change. Life will sometimes force us to look at ourselves and we have a choice as to whether we choose to deal with the issues or ignore them. I am pleased to say that over time those issues did get addressed and I share how in the coming chapters.

# Why?

Why is it so hard for me to let go?
You say come unto me all that labour,
I will give you rest
and show you my favour.

Rest is where I yearn to be
but first I have to bend my knees.
In prayer is where I find relief
but only when I truly believe.

So, bid me Lord to come to thee,
Not looking back on who I've been.
Help me Lord with my unbelief
To know that you have made me clean.

**H. Henry**

# Chapter Two

## What is Alignment?

I have spent some time sharing some very personal information and the question should be asked what all this has to do with alignment.

Alignment can be defined as: Arrangement in a straight line or in correct relative positions. A position of agreement or alliance. (www.oxfordlearnersdictionaries.com web.18 May 2020)

In order for something to be aligned, there needs to be awareness that it is not straight or not in the correct position. It needs to be lined up with something else. For example, the wheel of a car can be impacted by hitting a kerb or pothole that can result in the wheel becoming misaligned. If that does occur, then that will impact on the wear and tear of the tyres. It can also affect the steering of the vehicle. Misaligned tyres can also cause vibration in the steering wheel which makes the car more difficult to handle. In extreme cases, misalignment can result in a pull to one side causing the car not to drive in a straight line. Driving with misaligned tyres, particularly at speed, can be dangerous, especially if a blow-out should occur.

One can apply the principle of misalignment to life in a similar way. An external situation can impact upon a person's life so much so that it affects who they are, what they become and how they perceive themselves. This whole process is not necessarily intentional by any means, just as it is very unlikely that someone intentionally hits a kerb or pothole whilst driving.

These events usually occur by accident or through a circumstance beyond your control. It may be some time before you even realise how much damage has been caused to the vehicle. Initially, the damage may appear to be subtle, but over time you usually become aware that the car is not performing to its full potential. If you are not sure what is causing the problem, you are likely to go to a mechanic, explain the issues you are experiencing, and the mechanic is likely to undertake a diagnostic analysis to identify the problem. In this day and age, we are very blessed with technology and we may be inclined to check things out on Google. However, this is not a problem that can easily be resolved remotely. The car needs to be taken to a garage where the mechanic has access to the correct machinery and equipment to resolve the problem.

Similarly, when we hit our potholes in life, it is imperative we apply the same principle of identifying that something is misaligned within us. There is usually some indication; you know within yourself, when something is not quite right. You may have had those moments where you ask yourself questions like, Why do I react like that in those situations? or Why do I experience these emotions under these circumstances? or Why do I seem to attract the wrong people? or Why am I not like....?

Sometimes there are questions to which we just do not have the answers or are unable to articulate what is going on inside of us, but in all honesty, we can identify when something is not quite right.

It is imperative that when we are confronted with this uneasiness, we recognise that we have two options. We can either ignore it or continue to pretend to ourself and the world that all is well. To admit to ourselves that something is not quite right is the hardest thing to do as no one likes to feel vulnerable.

I remember how I felt when my friend told me that I never expressed my own opinion and when my other friend said she felt like I had a brick wall around me. They were both right. I was aware but did not know what to do with the information. As a Christian, I prayed about the matter often and there were many times when I cried and asked myself, what is wrong with me, and Why did God make me like this? Little did I know that this was going to be a journey of discovery, as I will explore later.

Acknowledgment can be defined as: To accept the truth or existence of something (www.oxforddictionaries.com web.18 May 2020)

Other synonyms include admission, confession, realization, awareness and appreciation. Once something has been acknowledged by an individual, it can then be addressed. It is virtually impossible to address an issue that you refuse to accept due to being in a state of denial. I was at the stage where I had accepted that I had issues that needed to be addressed, and God knew that I was now ready. This process involved aligning myself with the word of God. I will explain what that meant in reality for me.

The Bible is the written word of God and within it is the book of Proverbs. This book is written by the wisest man that has ever lived (apart from Jesus Christ). His name is king Solomon. The book of Proverbs is a book of instruction and contains many golden nuggets for life in general. I fully recommend reading and studying this book. Whether you believe in the Bible or not, one cannot deny the wisdom that is contained within it.

The opening chapter stipulates the following:

Proverbs 1:1-6

*These are the proverbs of King Solomon of Israel, David's son:*

*He wrote them to teach his people how to live – how to act in every circumstance, for he wanted them to be understanding, just and fair in everything they did.*

*"I want to make the simple-minded wise." he said. "I want to warn young men about some problems they will face.*

*I want those already wise to become the wiser and become leaders by exploring the depths of meaning in these nuggets of truth." How does one become wise? The first step is to trust and reverence the Lord. Only fools refuse to be taught.*

The final sentence highlights the difficulty in teaching a person something that he or she thinks he or she already knows.

One of my sons informed me that he was tutoring someone who believed she already knew the subject he was teaching. He stated that her methodology was incorrect. She had memorised formulae but did not understand the principles within the formula. Consequently, her strategy would work in some situations but not in others because she was not able to adapt the formula she had memorised.

After a few sessions with Alex, he had helped her to understand the principles of each formula and, once she understood and applied them, her overall grades began to improve. On her last test paper she scored 92% and since then has booked extra sessions with him. That is what can happen when we are willing to learn and apply golden nuggets to life in general.

There are many many more golden nuggets in Proverbs that are both timeless and applicable to life today.

Proverbs 6:6–11

> *Take a lesson from the ants, you lazy fellow. Learn from their ways and be wise.*
>
> *For though they have no king to make them work, yet they labour hard all summer, gathering food for the winter. But you-all you do is sleep. When will you wake up?*
>
> *"Let me sleep a little longer." Sure, just a little more.*
>
> *And as you sleep poverty creeps upon you like a robber and destroys you; want attacks you in full armour.*

As a child, I used to sit in the garden and watch the ants marching along like an army, collecting their food and taking it back to their nest. It is so true what king Solomon said. The ants are so regimental and precise, yet so tiny and insignificant and yet, as Solomon said, we can learn so much from their discipline and hard work.

Imagine, even the ants know that it is important to gather food in the summer to sustain them through the winter. Yet there are people who do not even think about a season when they may not be able to sustain themselves. Some are happy to spend in excess of their means and some, not thinking about the future, sleep their life away and remain in poverty. Even the ants know their purpose and in order to ensure their existence, they have to prepare for the future season. How much more us?

As I said, there are so many nuggets and not just in the book of Proverbs. The entire Bible is a whole collection of books, like a library that contains so much information and golden nuggets applicable to life today.

The late Dr Myles Munroe was a great preacher, teacher and speaker. He stated that, knowledge is information, understanding is comprehension and wisdom is the application.

(www.facebook.com/bureauofwisdom web May 18, 2020)

His definition is so simple yet very profound. We can all think of someone who may be very knowledgeable and intelligent but is unable to comprehend or translate that knowledge into common sense. Likewise, we can all think of someone who is able to comprehend or understand a situation but unable to apply the wisdom necessary to initiate change, despite the effort of others to enlighten them. Therefore, when one has information, comprehension and the desire to apply wisdom, then there is likely to be some change in behaviour.

I remember when a friend had left some food in the fridge for four days. He did not want to waste it. He was advised by an environmental health officer who happened to be in the vicinity and had studied food safety, not to eat the food as he would most likely end up with food poisoning.

The person received the information and then rejected the advice given and ate the food as he wanted to see what would happen. Well, he soon found out. He experienced severe food poisoning and then admitted that he should have listened. This is a typical example of someone who is well educated (to degree level) in his mid-forties and was clearly not exercising wisdom. Consequently he suffered as a consequence of his unwise decision. He was given the knowledge or information and clearly comprehended it, but refused to apply it to his circumstance, resulting in a display of the usual symptoms of severe food poisoning. Unfortunately, there are many of us who have behaved in this way and continue to act in a similar way, but thankfully many of us have also learned from our mistakes.

As previously stated, our lives can often be misaligned and just as the tyres on a vehicle may need to be realigned so too our lives. Our lives are too precious and time is too short to just carry on ignoring or denying that we are misaligned.

The reality of the situation is that misaligned lives can result in further damage over time, not only to you as an individual but potentially to others as well. It could cause devastating incidents resulting in collateral damage involving family, friends, colleagues or an innocent bystander that just happened to be in the way. We can also be easily influenced or manipulated in the opposite direction when we are misaligned as we are distracted or tempted onto a different route in life. This too can result in us not fulfilling our true potential or living an abundant life.

Alignment involves a process of being lined up with something else. In the case of the tyres of a vehicle it may need to be aligned with the laser beam of a machine. The misaligned wheels need to be measured against something, in order for it to be repositioned correctly. This process will involve some form of expenditure on the part of the individual who owns the vehicle. When a vehicle is in need of repair, the first thought that usually crosses the individuals mind is, How much is this going to cost and how long will I be without the vehicle? If we are willing to allow God to work on us, we need to be mindful; it will cost us something too. We also need to trust him to do the work just like we would trust the mechanic with our vehicle.

As a Christian I believe that God created us in His own image, we are not robots. We have the ability to think, feel, make decisions and learn from our experiences if we so choose. We are not just animals that operate in the realm of behavioural instincts. We are not here by accident or chance. Even before we were formed, the Bible says that He knew us. (Jeremiah 1:5)

Psalms 139: 13–18

> *You made all the delicate, inner parts of my body, and knit them together in my mother's womb.*

*Thank you for making me so wonderfully complex. It's amazing to think about. Your workmanship is marvellous-and how well I know it.*

*You were there while I was being formed in utter seclusion.*

*You saw me before I was born and scheduled each day of my life before I began to breathe. Every day was recorded in your book.*

*How precious it is Lord to realize that you are thinking about me constantly. I can't even count how many times a day your thoughts turn towards me.*

*And when I awaken in the morning, you are still thinking about me.*

Just think about this passage for a second. God thinks about us constantly even when we are not thinking about Him. God knows who we are; knows who we will become; knows what impact we will make in this life and who we will influence. He knew the potholes that we will encounter in life that cause us to be misaligned. He also knows that the time will come when we will need to be realigned or healed. This is usually a challenging time in our lives, but the choice is ours. Just like no one can force an individual to take their car in for repair despite advice or evidence that it is not driving to its full potential, no-one can force you to take action.

As John Heywood's proverb states: A man may well bring a horse to water, But he cannot make him drink without he will. (John Heywood proverbs collection 1546, www.writingexplained.org web May 18, 2020)

You can lead a horse to water but you cannot force it to drink, in today's terminology.

One of my friends has a saying, "You choose, until your last breath. You have the power to choose what course of action you want to take".

I remember the thought process that came into my mind with regards to my father. I tried so hard to persuade myself it was a bad idea to visit him and gave every reason possible as to why I should not have gone but instead, I chose to align myself with God's word.

Mark 12:31 (KJV)

*....Love your neighbour as you love yourself.*

Those words impacted my life as I knew I harboured bitterness and anger inside of me and I felt guilty. I did not know what to expect when I knocked on my father's door; it was a risk I had to take in obedience to God's word.

I had to step out and trust the Lord Jesus Christ. This was one of my first experiences of being aligned with His word. There was something to line up with and up to. I did not know how it would benefit me at the time but all I know is that when I came into alignment and adhered to what the word said, I believe my father and I have both benefitted. I was released from the guilt, bitterness and anger, and my father gained his daughter back. You can see how this could have panned out if I had chosen not to align with God's word. Another generation could have lost out on having a grandfather because there would have been no relationship.

Some people argue that God does not exist because he cannot be seen or touched. I once heard someone ask if you can physically touch an emotion. Can bitterness, anger, resentment or hatred be touched? The answer is, No. Do these emotions exist? The answer is, Yes, they do. How do we know? We feel these emotions inside of us and what is on the inside usually comes out. Sometimes you know if you are in the presence of someone who does not like you, or resents you. How? Because of their behaviour, attitude or the vibes that comes from them.

When I became a Christian, I felt the change inside of me and I knew that I was accepted for who I was and that I had been forgiven for my sins and for the offences I had caused to God. This only came about when I acknowledged that I was not living my life as God intended me to live it, which was and is in accordance with His word (The Bible).

It is interesting that the definition of sin is not only to cause offence to God but also to miss the mark. That mark is to live a life that is aligned with His word.

John 1:14 (KJV)

*And the Word was made flesh and dwelt among us, (and we beheld his glory, the glory as of the only begotten of the Father,) full of grace and truth.*

This verse and the whole first chapter of John's Gospel, talks about Jesus Christ. He was the overall embodiment of the Word of God. He is an example of the living Word of God.

This is endorsed further when the comment was made in

Matthew 3:16–17 (KJV)

*And Jesus, when He was baptized, went up straightway out of the water: and lo, the heavens opened unto Him and He saw the Spirit of God descending like a dove, and lighting*

> upon Him: And lo a voice from heaven saying, this is my beloved Son, in whom I am well pleased.

This was an outward confirmation by God that Jesus Christ was the ideal pattern of what it means to be a child of God. Jesus Christ had not missed the mark of what God intended Him to be.

Likewise, if you choose to be aligned with God's word and what He intends for you to be, you too can live your life to the full potential; as His child. Subsequently, you can experience peace, joy, fulfillment and satisfaction and it matters not what pothole you hit, you know you can always go back to the Creator and He will do the necessary repairs that will enable you to be realigned and get back on track.

The main expenditure may be your time, trust, obedience and faith. There also needs to be some agreement and proactivity on your part. Overall, I can truly say that it is well worth it.

Matthew 7:7 (KJV)

> Ask, and it shall be given you; seek, and ye shall find; knock, and it shall be opened unto you:

Just like you would ask a mechanic for a diagnosis and need to give permission for him to work on your vehicle, we need to ask God to work on us, as He will not force or impose Himself upon us.

If you are not willing to make the expenditure on repairing your vehicle, your vehicle will deteriorate and there will be long term damage. Similarly, in your life, if you blatantly know what God's word says and refuse to align with it, this could result in other parts of your life being affected, including feelings of stress, depression, feeling unfulfilled or devalued. All of which could affect your health and well-being because you have made the decision to pull against God's word or what He requires from you.

Whatever you choose to align yourself with will affect the destiny of your life and future.

Amos 3:3 (KJV)

*Can two walk together, except they be agreed?*

When it comes to alignment there has to be some form of agreement from both parties otherwise alignment cannot take place.

Many years ago, when farmers ploughed the land with oxen, they would have a wooden beam linking two of the same animals together to pull the load. This device was called a yoke and some cultures still adopt this strategy today. The animals would be yoked together and work in partnership together to complete the task. Each animal should be of a similar height so that there is no imbalance when pulling or linking them together.

Deuteronomy 22:10 (KJV)

*Thou shalt not plow with an ox and an ass together.*

To state the obvious, an ass is taller than an ox, which means there would be a difference in their height and strides. An ox is stronger than an ass and the yoke between them would not be equally balanced. This unequal distribution of the yoke will eventually cause damage to both of the animals as they would be out of sync and pulling against each other. Using this as an illustration, Jesus encourages us to be yoked to Him.

Matthew 11:28

> ....Come to me, and I will give you rest - all of you who work so hard beneath a heavy yoke. Wear my yoke - for it fits perfectly - and let me teach you; for I am gentle and humble, and you shall find rest for your souls; for I give you only light burdens.

Similarly, when we align and partner ourselves with Jesus Christ, we can be equally yoked to Him. Subsequently we walk in sync with him as we are joined together, pulling on the yoke with Him as He teaches us His word and truth. Thus, we find rest and our burden becomes easier and our load becomes lighter as He walks with us and we walk with Him.

1 Corinthians 6:17 (KJV)

> But he that is joined unto the Lord is one spirit.

If we choose to pull in the opposite direction, then clearly, we are aligning ourselves with the opposite of what God wants for us and therefore, we have to take responsibility for the choices we make.

2 Corinthians 6:14-18

> Don't be teamed with those who do not love the Lord, for what do the people of God have in common with the people of sin? How can light live with darkness?

*And what harmony can there be between Christ and the devil? How can a Christian be a partner with one who doesn't believe?*

*And what union can there be between God's temple and idols? For you are God's temple, the home of the living God, and God has said of you, "I will live in them and walk among them, I will be their God and they shall be my people."*

*That is why the Lord has said, "leave them; separate yourselves from them; don't touch their filthy things, and I will welcome you, and be a Father to you, and you will be my sons and daughters."*

The latter part of that Scripture demonstrates how we can be truly aligned with God and His word. As explained, we all have the ability to choose, but we also have to accept the consequences that come with the decisions we make.

Another step of alignment that took place in my life, funnily enough, was the second part of the message I was given regarding my father. Love your neighbour was the first part. The second part of the message was ... as yourself. Matthew 22:39 (KJV)

In the past I put everybody else above or before myself for fear of rejection and valued their opinions more than my own. I also erected walls to protect myself and keep other people at a safe distance. I did not understand I was doing this at the time; it had become a normal part of my life for so long. In all honesty, I really did not love myself. It was hard sometimes because like many other people I wore a mask. On the outside I looked fine and acted fine but sometimes inside I asked myself what was wrong with me.

It was only when I had left home to study that I began to find out who I really was. There was nobody telling me where to go and what to do and I inevitably had a great deal of freedom. Although this was an exciting time of my life, there were other times where I felt trepidation. I was on my own and was totally responsible for myself. In reality I did not truly know who I was. I was now independent, in an independent world I had to navigate in order to survive.

As a student I realised that I could not hide in the crowd and I had to express my opinions in written assignments in a small seminar group or whilst I was at my work placement. It was so difficult; I doubted myself but had to appear confident. I had a few friends to whom I became very close and once we left the halls of residence, we decided to live together for a couple of years and would sometimes study together.

This was a huge help as I began to realise that my opinions did matter and that I did have something to say of value and that others appreciated. I also became involved in a local church and the Christian Union on campus. This presented other opportunities for me to develop more confidence as I was given the responsibility of being a worship leader and group leader along with my friend. I could not hide anymore as people were relying on me to undertake responsibilities almost every week. I accepted the new challenges and over time grew in confidence. There were some very special people that the Lord Jesus Christ used to help me come out of my shell and love myself and to believe what the word of God says in Psalms 139 (quoted previously). Each of us is unique and has been designed individually. Not even identical twins have the same finger prints even though they have come from the same fertilised egg. How awesome is that!

Once I began to accept and love myself the way God loved me, I no longer accepted the labels people placed on me. I accepted the value God placed on me and that changed my whole perspective of who I was and who He had created me to be.

We live in a selfie culture where people are encouraged to post things on social media - thus giving someone else the opportunity to validate or approve what they see by making a comment or sending a 'like'. I am so glad that God sees us and loves us for who we are. We do not need to receive a like or a post from God because He has already given us His approval when He created us.

When any business is established, one of the key elements that is examined is, what makes that business different to their competitors? In other words, what is their USP - unique selling point. Well, in our case, what makes us different from any other individual is that we have our own USP. We are a Unique and Special Person in God's eyes. There will never ever be another ……………………………………… (insert your name) and that is one reason, amongst others, why you should love and celebrate you.

It is also imperative to state that it is very difficult to accept the love of someone else when you do not accept or love yourself. It is virtually impossible because you never feel good enough or, if someone tells you he/she loves you; you are unlikely to believe it.

Alternatively, your perception could be skewed on the basis that you think he/she is more valuable than you and therefore you believe everything that is said. Eventually you can find yourself in a situation where you are in a relationship that is imbalanced and unfortunately sometimes abusive, synonymous to being unequally yoked.

It can also be difficult to accept the love of God too, in that you just do not believe that you are lovable, precious and special in His eyes. As a result, you just continue on the tread mill of what life throws at you rather than seeking to fulfill your potential and utilise the gifts and talents that were given to you to help you achieve your purpose.

## You Can't Have Me!

You can't have me!
Was it you that died for me?
No, it wasn't you,
You're my enemy!

Go ahead and fight me,
Because it's not me you're fighting,
It's the greater in me,
that will give you a good hiding!

I have no power no strength of my own,
But I know when I'm weak, I'm not alone!
It's then I'm made strong by the one I am yoked to.
You know his name ... Jesus, the true Lion
whose roar you're afraid of.

Remember when you saw him hung on the cross,
Your kingdom laughed with relief and thought all was lost.
It was finished alright, the very work he came to do.
To pay a ransom for mankind, yes you know it is true!

But foolishly you thought you had won the victory,
death He has conquered and took back the keys!

No name is greater. No not on earth above or beneath,
The name of Jesus my Stronghold, Conqueror,
Everlasting Father and Prince of all Peace!

H. Henry

# Chapter Three

## What about the Assignment?

The definition of assignment is: a task, or piece of work that has been allocated to someone as part of a job, course or study. (www.oxfordlearnersdictionaries.com web.21 May 2020)

It can be synonymous to having a duty, function, mission, commission, occupation or responsibility.

We can undertake assignments in our lives but not necessarily to our full potential. I stress this because a car with misaligned tyres will still drive but not to its full potential. When the tyres have been placed back into alignment, it is so much easier to drive and the car operates much more smoothly. How much more our lives if we undertake assignments when we are in alignment with what God has intended for us.

The assignment becomes much more manageable and easier to handle because we recognise that we are operating in alignment with our Creator and what He has created us to do. He has also given us His manual; God's written word, the Bible. In addition to this, there has to be an element of trust, obedience and faith in His word and a belief that He does not want to harm us and knows what is best for us.

Jeremiah 29:11

*For I know the plans I have for you, says the Lord. They are plans for good and not for evil, to give you a future and a hope.*

When we encounter *potholes* in life, even though they may be challenging, difficult, painful or we feel out of our depth, to choose to align with this particular Scripture is powerful. You know the outcome will be positive as He said, *...plans for good and not for evil, to give you a future and a hope.*

That changes the whole perspective of what can often be difficult and challenging situations. God has all bases covered to protect us and to ensure that our outcome is positive, even though it may not and very often does not, appear like that at the time. That is the time when we need to apply faith and trust and remind God of what His word says. The alternative when you hit that *pothole,* is to feel defeated, depressed and lose all hope for the future. Now, with which one would you choose to align yourself with?

I know this is so much easier said than done. I remember when my vehicle broke down a few years ago. The timing belt snapped and the vehicle was completely immobilised. I called the RAC® and the gentleman explained that he would have to tow the vehicle as there was no power at all to enable the car to drive. He connected the tow bar device and gave me specific instructions that I had to remain behind the steering wheel, but I should let him have complete control while he towed the vehicle.

I had been driving for over twenty-five years and to sit behind the wheel of a vehicle and not do anything was extremely difficult. In fact, I found it impossible and kept putting my foot on the brake and trying to steer. I had only been towed for a few seconds when the RAC driver pulled over, came out of his vehicle and said to me, *"If you don't stop putting the brakes on you will cause an accident"* and then said I had to trust him to take full control. It was challenging but when he mentioned accident, I thought to *myself* I must keep off the brakes and trust him.

As I was behind the steering wheel the Lord spoke into my heart and said that is how He wanted us to be as His children. To allow Him to be in the driving seat of our lives and take full control and for us to trust Him.

In that situation, my assignment was to be still and to trust the driver in the other vehicle to take me to my destination safely. Sometimes it is so hard to keep still and trust especially when you are not the driver but that is what God wants. It sounds ironic that your assignment can be to *keep still* but sometimes that is all He wants us to do.

Psalms 46:10 (KJV)

*Be still and know that I am God.*

It is during those times of stillness and quietness that He can really communicate with us as to what He wants us to do, where He wants us to go and basically reveal to us His assignments. It can also be a time where He can reveal His awesome power by bringing about a resolution without our intervention. Then we too can stand in awe and thank Him for what He has done or is doing independently of us.

There is a prophet, Elijah, to whom God wanted to reveal Himself. 1 Kings 19: 11-13

*"Go out and stand before me on a mountain," the Lord told him. And as Elijah stood there the Lord passed by, and a*

*mighty windstorm hit the mountain; it was such a terrible blast that the rocks were torn loose, but the Lord was not in the wind. After the wind, there was an earthquake, but the Lord was not in the earthquake.*

*And after the earthquake, there was a fire, but the Lord was not in the fire. And after the fire, there was the sound of a gentle whisper.*

*When Elijah heard it, he wrapped his face in his scarf and went out and stood at the entrance of the cave. And a voice said, "Why are you here, Elijah?"*

God does not always speak to us in the drama of our situation. Can you imagine Elijah watching all that drama unfolding before his eyes? There is no doubt it was dramatic, but God spoke in that small still voice and sometimes He speaks to us in that way too.

The background to this scenario was that God had just used Elijah to complete an assignment. His task was to challenge the extremely wicked and evil attitudes of the people initiated by the ruling monarchy. He successfully eradicated the problem in the short-term as God used him to demonstrate His miraculous power. Shortly afterwards, his life was now threatened by the evil queen, Jezebel, who abhorred him and sent a death threat to him. He fell into a state of fear and depression after being on the mountain top (literally) performing great miracles. Now he was scared, which is understandable under the circumstances.

Elijah was now misaligned. However, God reminded Elijah that He was still in the driving seat of his situation and that there was no need for him (Elijah) to worry. Although Elijah felt alone and isolated during this time, God reminded him that there were another seven thousand people in Israel who had not submitted themselves to the immoral demands of the monarchy at that time.

The full story can be found in 1 Kings Chapters 18 and 19.

Once again, this highlights how relevant and applicable the word of God is in that it shows the reality of the different feelings and emotions we all experience in life when exposed to challenging circumstances. Sometimes we are on the metaphorical mountain top and other times we are in the valley. God reminds us that if we are willing to align ourselves with Him, He can and will bring us through the difficult times.

Deuteronomy 31:6

> ...*Be strong. Be courageous. Do not be afraid of them for the Lord your God will be with you. He will neither fail you nor forsake you.*

There is another situation in the Bible when a king of Israel, Jehoshaphat, was intimidated and feared defeat when threatened by his enemies. The nation of Judah hit a *pothole;* they believed they were about to be annihilated. They had to choose their response and cried out to God, their Creator, the only one who they believed could help to resolve the situation; not knowing what that resolution might be.

2 Chronicles 20:2–4

> *Word reached Jehoshaphat that "a vast army is marching against you from beyond the Dead Sea, from Syria. It is already at Hazazon-tamar" (also called Engedi).*
>
> *Jehoshaphat was badly shaken by this news and determined to beg for help from the Lord; so he announced that all the*

> people of Judah should go without food for a time in penitence and intercession before God.
>
> People from all across the nation came to Jerusalem to plead unitedly with Him.

Then the answer came:

2 Chronicles 20:15–17

> ...The Lord says, "Don't be afraid. Don't be paralyzed by this mighty army. For the battle is not yours, but God's.
>
> Tomorrow, go down and attack them. You will find them coming up the slopes of Ziz at the end of the valley that opens up into the wilderness of Jeruel.
>
> But you will not need to fight. Take your places; stand quietly and see the incredible rescue operation God will perform for you, O people of Judah and Jerusalem. Don't be afraid or discouraged. Go out there tomorrow, for the Lord is with you."

Imagine for one moment you are about to be attacked by your enemies and their army is much greater than yours. In your opinion you have no chance of success. You realise that the only option you really have is to pray because, as it stands, everything else is out of your control.

When our back is against the wall, in a moment of desperation, whether we believe in God or not, we automatically cry out to God. Especially if we just do not know where to turn or what to do. It is as if there is something innate within us that we automatically cry out to Him.

In this example, Jehoshaphat recognised that he was not able to suddenly increase his army as he did not have the resources. He could not control the actions of his enemy, but he recognised that he could call the nation to pray. He chose his response to a dire situation and the prayer was heard. When Jehoshaphat was given the answer, some would suggest that he was crazy to accept that answer and be a sitting duck. However, he allowed God to be in the driving seat and the expenditure that he had to make was to trust God, believe the word that was given and stand still. I am sure that was not easy but in this case he accepted the challenge and the assignment. The conclusion is that king Jehoshaphat and his army survived.


2 Chronicles 20:22

*And at the moment they began to sing and to praise, the Lord caused the armies of Ammon, Moab and Mount Seir to begin fighting among themselves and they destroyed each other.*


This example reminds me of a book I recently read that made reference to the Second World War. The Germans had advanced across France and Belgium rapidly. The French defenses had been broken down. The decision was made to evacuate the Western forces, but this expedition could only take place at Dunkirk, which was already under threat by the enemy.

But Britain had a godly Sovereign. Seeing this situation developing, His Majesty, King George VI, requested that Sunday, 26 May should be observed as a National Day of Prayer. In a stirring broadcast, he called the people of Britain and of the Empire to commit their cause to God. Together with members of the cabinet, the king attended

Westminster Abbey, whilst millions of his subjects in all parts of the Commonwealth and Empire flocked to the churches to join in prayer. Britain was given inspiring leadership in those days, and her people responded immediately when this kind of initiative was taken. The whole nation was at prayer that Sunday. The scene outside Westminster Abbey was remarkable; photographs show long queues of people who could not even get in, the Abbey was so crowded. So much so, that the following morning the Daily Sketch exclaimed, *Nothing like it has ever happened before.* (Gardner 2003: The Trumpet Sounds for Britain, p49)

The prayers were answered in the form of at least three miracles.

The first was that for some reason Hitler overruled his generals and halted the advance of his armoured columns at the very point when they could have proceeded and brought about the British army's annihilation. They were only ten miles away. (Gardner 2003: The Trumpet Sounds for Britain, p49)

"I have talked to officers and men who have got safely back to England, and all of them tell of these two phenomena. The first was the great storm which broke over Flanders on Tuesday, 28 May. The second was the great calm which settled on the English Channel the days following.

Officers of high rank do not hesitate to put down the deliverance of the British Expeditionary Force to the fact of the nation being at prayer on Sunday, 26 May, two days before that great storm in Flanders and the calm that came over the Channel.

Mr Churchill, when he chose 4 June as the occasion for making a statement to the House of Commons, spoke with a voice charged with emotion when he reported that, rather than 20,000, or 30,000 men being re-embarked,

"335,000 men had been carried out of the jaws of death and shame to their native land."

He referred to what happened as "a miracle of deliverance". (Gardner 2003: The Trumpet Sounds for Britain, pp 51-52)

We do not hear of this often when we remember those who fought in the Second World War. I would recommend reading the book as it gives a comprehensive account of the events that occurred. The British and their allies could not control what was going on in the German camp, but they could control what was happening in their camp. The Monarchy called the nation to pray and whether one believes that prayer can have an impact or not, one cannot deny the events that happened afterwards.

Like Jehoshaphat, the British army was about to be annihilated but the weather conditions changed and prevented this from occurring. Hitler was unable to send in an air attack due to extreme weather conditions. This enabled the British soldiers to travel to Dunkirk where they could be rescued. Secondly, after that extreme storm there was another extreme weather condition. The English Channel was extremely calm, this enabled every floating vessel possible whether small or great to travel across to Dunkirk and rescue what was left of the British army. As a result, over 335,000 men were saved. The king must have had some faith to request the whole nation to pray and he must have had an expectation that the prayer would be heard but not knowing how the prayer was going to be answered. There was clearly an alignment with the word of God.

2 Chronicles 7:14 (KJV)

*If my people that are called by my name, shall humble themselves, and pray, and seek my face, and turn from their wicked ways; then will I hear from heaven, and will forgive their sin, and will heal their land.*

My husband has a saying that is very simple yet very profound. *Deal with the things that you can control as you cannot control the actions of other people.* When I truly comprehended what he meant by this and applied his advice I literally felt empowered and liberated and more in control of situations.

Prior to having this understanding, I would spend hours and hours worrying about issues and feeling guilty; hoping that I had not hurt the feelings of others, or that I had not caused them offence. I was still trapped in the mindset of wanting to please everyone I could, at the expense of myself as the word, *No,* did not exist in my vocabulary.

I am not saying that I do not care about the feelings and emotions of others with regards to what I may say or do. What I am saying is that I have learned to put boundaries in place and not allow others to manipulate or control my actions or behaviour. I did not apply this until well into my forties but as they say, *Better late than never.*

I eventually learned to take ownership and responsibility for my actions and decisions and learned to deal with the things that I could control. I learned this the hard way.

I had just started a new job and I was in a situation where I had to prepare a report for the court regarding the welfare of a baby. It was my first court hearing in my new role. After a thorough assessment of the case, I had made a recommendation to the court that the mother should be given the opportunity to go to a mother-and-baby unit where she could be assessed under supervision to determine whether she could care for her child or not.

The usual protocol of the court was that the person representing the welfare of the children (myself) would give evidence last. I was called to the stand and was the first to give evidence, something for which I was not mentally prepared. I started off confidently but as the cross examination continued, I began to lose confidence and focus and, literally, at one stage froze and could not answer the questions. I felt humiliated and embarrassed in front of all the solicitors and barristers and the Judge. However, the one thing I learned from that experience was that I would never make a recommendation or decision without being able to explain why I had come to that conclusion. I took responsibility for my actions as I was to blame for not adequately preparing myself for any possible eventuality.

There have been numerous cases following that one where I have had to give evidence, but I can assure you that a situation like that never ever occurred again because I learned from that first experience. If I could not defend what I was recommending, then I did not recommend it. I learned to take ownership for the decisions I make, and chose to learn from each experience. It is in these situations that we can grow and develop our character and find out who we really are and what we really believe.

God will prepare you or has already prepared you for your assignment. As previously stated, He created us, designed us, and gave us our personality, gifts and talents. He knew us before we knew ourselves. Therefore, what we do is no surprise to Him, even though it may be a surprise to us. All we have to do is ensure that we are in alignment with His word. We also need to know what the word says and choose to align with it.

As previously stated, God speaks to us in many ways. It may be a still quiet voice directly into our heart or through His written word. It may be through a friend, nature, a book or a song. It may be through a preacher, a prophet or a film.

The point I am making is that God is not prescriptive and does not have a specific formula when communicating with us. As I previously stated, we usually know when He is speaking as we feel a *probing* inside. What is communicated is in alignment with His word. It is then your choice whether you decide to respond to the probing of God's word or whether you decide to ignore it.

Hebrews 3:15

> But now is the time. Never forget the warning, "today if you hear God's voice speaking to you, do not harden your hearts against him, as the people of Israel did when they rebelled against him in the desert."

When we agree to come into alignment with God's word then great things can be accomplished. If we refuse to come into alignment, the outcome of the assignment could be very different but there would still be an outcome. If we refuse the assignment then God will sometimes allow us to take a detour and show us the error of our ways. He may even give us another opportunity but this is not always the case.

Jonah was a man who God clearly gave an assignment. He was told to go to the people of Nineveh and warn them of God's impending judgment. Jonah was afraid to deliver the message and so took a detour.

Jonah 1:3

> But Jonah was afraid to go and ran away from the Lord. He went down to the seacoast, to the port of Joppa, where he found a ship leaving for Tarshish. He bought a ticket, went on board and climbed down into the dark hold of the ship to hide there from the Lord.

God watched him and allowed him to take the detour. Many of us sometimes take detours, as we pull in the opposite direction of where God wants us to go. In the case of Jonah, it results in him going to a different location and getting on board a boat. There is then a tempestuous storm that results in him being thrown overboard and collected by a huge fish. Jonah eventually acknowledges he has disobeyed God and is spat out by the fish. It is only at that stage that he accepts the assignment he had been asked to do in the first place.

Jonah 3:3–4

*So, Jonah obeyed, and went to Nineveh. Now Nineveh was a very large city, with many villages around it – so large that it would take three days to walk through it.*

*But the very first day when Jonah entered the city and began to preach, the people repented. Jonah shouted to the crowds that gathered around him, "Forty days from now Nineveh will be destroyed."*

Although Jonah's first response was not in alignment with God's request, God still gave him an opportunity to fulfil his assignment. This is similar to the SatNav we use in our vehicles. Sometimes when we take a wrong turn, we see the SatNav recalculating to get us back on course for our destination. God is merciful and patient in that he does not abandon us if we take a detour as long as we are willing to accept the consequences of our actions. If we are willing to repent and come back into alignment with Him, then He may give us another opportunity to fulfil our assignment.

There may be other times when we miss the opportunity and God might pass the assignment onto to someone else who is willing and available. Mordecai believed this when the Jews were under threat in Shushan. The Jewish queen was told she could either reveal her identity and help to save all the Jews or she could keep quiet but if she did then God would use someone else to undertake the assignment to deliver them (Esther 4:13–14). I explore this in greater detail later.

The word of God is like a seed and each seed has an assignment. The outcome of His word depends upon how we respond to it and how we nurture it. Either way, there will always be an outcome. A seed can only grow under the right conditions. It usually needs to be buried into the ground, watered and kept in the right environment. If it is looked after correctly, it will grow; if not, it will die.

This is illustrated in the parable Jesus tells to his disciples in

Matthew 13:2–9

*A farmer was sowing grain in his fields.*

*As he scattered the seed across the ground, some fell beside a path, and the birds came and ate it.*

*And some fell on rocky soil where there was little depth of earth; the plants sprang up quickly enough in the shallow soil,*

*But the hot sun soon scorched them and they withered and died, for they had so little root.*

*Other seeds fell among thorns, and the thorns choked out the tender blades.*

*But some fell on good soil and produced a crop that was thirty, sixty, and even a hundred times as he had planted.*

*If you have ears, listen.*

His disciples then asked him to explain what he meant by that parable.

Matthew 13:18–23

*Now here is the explanation of the story I told you about the farmer planting grain:*

*The hard path where some of the seeds fell represents the heart of a person who hears the Good News about the Kingdom and doesn't understand it; then Satan comes and snatches away the seeds from his heart.*

*The shallow, rocky soil represents the heart of a man who hears the message and receives it with real joy, but he doesn't have much depth in his life, and the seeds don't root very deeply, and after a while when trouble comes, or persecution begins because of his beliefs, his enthusiasm fades, and he drops out.*

*The ground covered with thistles represents a man who hears the message, but the cares of this life and his longing for money choke out God's Word, and he does less and less for God.*

*The good ground represents the heart of a man who listens to the message and understands it and goes out and brings thirty, sixty, or even a hundred others into the Kingdom.*

We should always be mindful and ask ourselves the question have we provided the right soil and created the right environment for the seed (Word) to bring forth fruit in our lives.

All the *potholes* we encounter in life help to develop our character and help us to grow. These experiences can also help equip us to fulfill our assignments.

Diamonds and coal start off as different kinds of carbon under the ground but after a great deal of time, pressure and heat, that same piece of carbon turns into a beautiful diamond. John Platt, Do diamonds really come from coal? (www.mnn.com/stories web 21 May 2020)

Life can sometimes feel quite pressured and sometimes we find ourselves in situations where we feel like we are in the heat of the fire.

However, these experiences help us to become like a diamond in God's eyes. A diamond that sparkles and radiates beauty. When that diamond is lined up with the light of His word, you see the true beauty that is reflected and the impact that beauty has as it shines and twinkles in the atmosphere.

Matthew 5:14-16

> *You are the world's light – a city on a hill glowing in the night for all to see. Don't hide your light. Let it shine for all; let your good deeds glow for all to see, so that they will praise your heavenly Father.*

God created us to shine so do not hide from this world, shine like the stars shine bright at night in the sky above, as each and every one of those stars radiate beauty and each of those stars are different and unique.

Psalms 149:4 (KJV)

*For the LORD taketh pleasure in his people: he will beautify the meek with salvation.*


Imagine God taking pleasure in his people. He delights in us, loves us and accepts us for who we are, when we choose to line up with His word. For those of us who are parents, I can only liken this to when our children are involved in an activity that brings us pleasure. You just stand there in awe as you lovingly gaze at your child, enjoying the moment with them. If you do not have any children, then it may be somebody else's child or something you personally find pleasurable.

Psalms 149:4 goes on to say that *"he will beautify the meek* (those who are humble) *with salvation."* This means He allows His people to glisten, glow and shimmer with the light of His victory, prosperity, health and welfare as they experience complete deliverance from things that once held them in bondage. This beauty is then on display for others to see. That is why when someone accepts Jesus Christ into their life and begins to live in alignment with His word other people see that the person's life has changed.

2 Corinthians 5:17 (KJV)

*Therefore, if any man be in Christ, he is a new creature: old things are passed away; behold, all things become new.*


Some people may say that they know of people who profess to be Christians, but their lives do not reflect that of a Christian as stipulated in the word of God. Note what the Scripture says, *if any man be **IN** Christ, he is a new creature*. To be in something means to be surrounded or enclosed by something or in this case someone else. You are either surrounded by Him and abiding in Him or you are not, just like you are either in a boat or abiding in a boat or you are not. You cannot be experiencing being in and out of a boat at the same time. Jesus explained this further to his disciples.

John 15:4-6 (Jesus speaking)

> *Take care to live in me, and let me live in you. For a branch can't produce fruit when severed from the vine. Nor can you be fruitful apart from me.*
>
> *Yes, I am the Vine; you are the branches. Whoever lives in me and I in him shall produce a large crop of fruit. For apart from me you can't do a thing.*
>
> *If anyone separates from me, he is thrown away like a useless branch, withers and is gathered into a pile with all the others and burned...*

I am very passionate about gardening. One does not, however, need to be passionate about gardening to know that if a branch is disconnected from a tree it will eventually wither and die. This is the same for any plant or flower that is disconnected from the main source. Jesus is clearly saying that if we are not connected to Him, we will be unable to produce fruit and we become useless and serve no purpose. This will be explored a little further later on in this book.

## The Cares of Life

*The cares life brings heavy distress*
*It's only then, you long for my heavenly rest*
*Lay them down and lean on my breast*
*I know what to do for your very best*

*Fear has torment, that's not from me.*
*It will toss you and turn you and then fill you with unbelief*

*Trust in me I have healing in my wings*
*The work I do in you, will have you to win!*
*An overcomer I've made you and light to this world.*

*Don't let the cares of life pull you down*
*Hope in me, seek me with your whole heart*
*and I will be found!*

**H. Henry**

# Chapter Four

## The Reality of Being Assigned

There is a man called Moses in the Bible (Exodus 2) who started off his life at a time of mass genocide. His people (the Israelites) were in slavery to the Egyptian Empire. The Egyptians felt threatened that the Israelites were multiplying too quickly and would eventually overthrow them. Consequently, the Egyptians enforced a strategy where all male children were to be killed at birth.

Like any mother, Moses' mother could not bear to see her baby son killed so she hid him for three months. He was then placed in a basket and floated down a riverbank. He was found by Pharaoh's daughter whose father ironically had implemented the legislation that the male babies should be killed. Fortunately, she rescued Moses, cared for him and raised him as her own child. He was in a very privileged position as he was raised as an Egyptian and benefitted from all the trappings and luxuries of being an Egyptian Prince. It was also hard for him because he saw his people enslaved and the cruelty they endured as they were oppressed by the ruling empire at that time.

One day when Moses observed one of the Israelites being treated unjustly, he subsequently lashed out and it resulted in the slave-master being killed. Thus, Moses fled for his life at the age of forty (Acts 7:23) as he knew that he would be punished as a result of this crime. He left behind his home, family and security.

Moses hit a *pothole* in his life and literally had to start his whole life again; this time in the land of Midian as a shepherd. Now some would say that was a demotion considering where Moses was coming from, but he was now married, had a child and was probably just getting on with his life as many of us do when we are content and wanting to just survive.

The *pothole* that Moses encountered in his life was part of his preparation for a future assignment. He was called to go back to Egypt, the land that he knew so well. He understood the intricacies of the empire, the politics, the leadership, the infrastructure and the oppression of his people from which he had escaped both as a child and as an adult.

When God called Moses to undertake the assignment of being a freedom fighter for the people, Moses' response was:

Exodus 3:11-12

*"But I'm not the person for a job like that." Moses exclaimed.*

*Then God told him, "I will certainly be with you, this is the proof that I am the one who is sending you: When you have led the people out of Egypt, you shall worship God here upon this mountain."*

Moses then responded: Exodus 4:1

*But Moses said, "They will not believe me. They won't do what I tell them to. They'll say "Jehovah" never appeared to you."*

Despite God's attempts to reassure Moses over and over again by demonstrating His power in different ways, Moses was still not convinced he was the one for the assignment.

Exodus 4:10-16

> *But Moses pleaded, "O Lord, I'm just not a good speaker. I never have been, and I'm not now, even after you have spoken to me, for I have a speech impediment."*
>
> *"Who makes mouths?" Jehovah asked him. "Isn't it I, the Lord? Who makes a man so that he can speak or not speak, see or not see, hear or not hear?*
>
> *Now go ahead and do as I tell you, for I will help you to speak well, and I will tell you what to say."*
>
> *But Moses said, "Lord please. Send someone else."*
>
> *Then the Lord became angry. "All right," he said, "your brother, Aaron, is a good speaker. And he is coming here to look for you and will be very happy when he finds you.*
>
> *So I will tell you what to tell him, and I will help both of you to speak well, and I will tell you what to do."*

Moses reacted like any of us would. He immediately thought he was not good enough. He was not the person for the assignment; somehow God had made a mistake by appointing him to this assignment.

At that point Moses had a choice. He could have ignored all that God had said and just got on with his life or he could respond and accept the assignment he had been given. Moses eventually aligned his will with God's will and put his confidence in the one who said, *"I will be with thee."* In accepting the challenge, Moses became one of the greatest freedom fighters that has ever lived, as the Bible recounts the events of what happened to the Egyptian Empire and the nation of Israel at that time.

In addition to this Moses' time living in Midian (mountains and deserts) prepared him well for the evacuation of the nation of Israel out of Egypt, as they spent a long time in the very region in which he had previously spent forty years living and surviving.

As with all assignments there is a process that takes place. There is an identification of the assignment. A person either accepts or rejects the assignment and there is usually an awareness of who has allocated the assignment. Once this process takes place and there is an agreement, there is then an element of accountability on both the assignee (the person responsible for undertaking the assignment) and the assignor (the person who has appointed you to the task). Basically, each of those parties has a right to hold the other accountable.

In the case of Moses, once he aligned with the will of God, he accepted the assignment from the assignor (God). God was now accountable for what He said He would do and Moses was now responsible for undertaking the task as the designated assignee.

As with Moses, when we accept our assignment from God, there is an element of accountability. This takes the focus off us and places it on Almighty God. This enables us to recognise that He has equipped us to deal with the task He has entrusted unto us and reassures us that we will have all the resources that we need to fulfill the assignment. Despite this, we still need to show an element of accountability by having a level of faith, trust and confidence that He is more than able to supply what we need.


Ephesians 3:20 (KJV)

*Now unto him that is able to do exceedingly, abundantly above all that we ask or think, according to the power which worketh in us.*

This reminds us that God is able to go *above and beyond* our expectations. We should not limit Him. It is His power that is at work in us. He is therefore, able to do much more than we can ever think or ask or imagine as He is the God who has no limits. He will not set us up to fail because we are working on His behalf.

God demonstrated His awesome power to me prior to my marriage. As a child, I said to myself that I did not want to get married. Partly because of what I experienced through my parents' divorce and partly because of the unresolved issues I had at the time, including lack of trust and confidence.

However, I did have the opportunity to meet somebody at my local church. We were initially good friends. This proved very beneficial as it provided a very solid foundation for our future and also enabled me to address many unresolved issues over a period of time. I remember having very lengthy conversations with my friend and it took me some time to share my childhood experiences and other experiences with him, and how they had impacted upon my life.

During this time, I felt very vulnerable as I was opening up my emotions. I realised that as I began to open up, I developed a sense of trust. I did not experience rejection but acceptance for who I was. This proved to be one of the most challenging assignments of my life. Looking back now I realise I was being prepared to marry my friend.

At the time of our engagement my fiancé was unemployed and had been for a while. He was diligently seeking employment, but nothing had come to fruition. We were due to get married six months later. I am sure that some people thought it was unwise to get engaged, particularly as I was the only one who was employed at the time, but we decided to trust God.

I remember spending some time in prayer and fasting; abstaining from food for a few days and really focusing on God's word. During this time of prayer, God showed me the Scripture in Ephesians 3:20, *Now unto him that is able...* I remember looking at the definition of each of the words: able, exceedingly, abundantly above all that we could ask or think.

God was showing me that He is infinite, He has no limits, He has the ability to go beyond our expectations and our abilities. I am still in awe of this Scripture because nineteen days after we were engaged, my fiancé was successful in securing full-time employment. He worked for that company in various capacities for over twenty-three years and whilst there, they paid for him to complete a degree. That is the God we serve. He exceeded our expectations and is faithful to His word.

While engaged, we undertook marital counseling. It proved to be extremely beneficial as it allowed us to delve deep into our childhood experiences, our values and our attitude towards finances and other potential issues. We also discussed communication, children, work ethics and our core beliefs and goals. It was a time of laying the foundation for our future together and as far as I can recall, there was no stone that was left unturned. This really helped to cement our relationship and our marriage as there were no unexpected surprises once we were married.

My husband is now a Pastor and his background is in building studies. He said something very pertinent recently that I had not thought about before. He stated that when a building is being erected, it has to be built on a solid foundation. It takes a great deal of effort and time to dig deep and lay a foundation. As the digging takes place, sometimes things are uncovered that may need to be removed or things may need to be added in order to ensure that the foundation is solid. However, no one ever comes along and admires a foundation. Even before the building has been erected, no one gives it a compliment or ever says that this is a beautiful foundation. When the building has actually been erected on the foundation, that is when the compliments come; Oh, what a beautiful building. It's amazing isn't it, look at the structure, look at the shape of it.

This reminds me of a parable that Jesus tells in Matthew 7:24–28

> *All who listen to my instructions and follow them are wise, like a man who builds his house on solid rock.*
>
> *Though the rain comes in torrents, and the floods rise and the storm winds beat against his house, it won't collapse, for it is built upon rock.*
>
> *But those who hear my instructions and ignore them are foolish, like a man who builds his house on sand.*
>
> *For when the rains and floods come, and storm winds beat against his house, it will fall with a mighty crash.*

This is another *nugget* from the Bible. When a house is built on a solid foundation it can stand the test of time. There are houses today that are hundreds of years old still standing on the same foundation.

Before one is able to purchase a house, the mortgage lender will request that certain searches are undertaken. One of the searches is to ensure that there has been no mining in the vicinity that might compromise the foundation of the house. If there has been a significant amount of mining in the area, then these abandoned mine shafts could cause subsidence or, even worse, collapse or cave-in taking everything that is built upon it, with it.

I have seen horror stories on the television where some properties have been literally swallowed up by sinkholes because the foundation was not safe and secure. To see the devastation that has been caused is traumatic for the victims. In some cases, there was previous evidence that something was not right with the property.

Some homeowners observed a series of internal and external cracks before the devastation occurred. There have been occasions where my husband and I have viewed potential properties to purchase, and he has instantly observed cracks in the brickwork and sloping floors through his knowledge and experience whereas I have been totally oblivious to it.

A foundation that is not solid is a dangerous foundation and this is applicable to life in general. This could relate to marriage, friendships, starting up a business or anything else that requires some kind of investment.

If mortgage companies require searches to satisfy whether they would mortgage a property, then how much more should we research before we decide to invest in whatever we are thinking to be involved in. Once the mortgage company is satisfied with the searches, they are usually happy to lend on the property and release the necessary funds.

Likewise, appropriate research enables us to determine the quality of a foundation and we can then decide if we want to make further investment. Therefore, part of that research might be to ask and seek the answers to various questions like: What do I know about this person? What are his and my values regarding finances, family, career, beliefs? Is he responsible? Are there any unresolved issues within me? All of this should be underpinned with asking God to direct the path of our lives, as He also knows the desire of our hearts.

When we ask such questions, it focuses our minds and as a result helps us to assess how we can achieve what we want to accomplish in our lives. Therefore, we are not just hoping that we will achieve these goals, but we become intentional about achieving them. This also allows God to address any issues that may prevent us from achieving them.

There are countries that are subject to hurricane seasons and it is very sad to see the devastation that such hurricanes cause. In some cases, houses are totally destroyed and in other cases, they have been damaged but they are still standing.

This can be likened to when the storms or challenges of life hit. We may encounter some damage, but we are still standing. This is very much dependent on the foundation on which we choose to build.

Psalms 18:2(KJV)

*The LORD is my rock, and my fortress, and my deliverer; my God, my strength, in whom I will trust;*

In contrast to rock, sand is very unstable. In fact, it is not even a foundation. Sand is made up of many loose granular substances that are the result of the wearing down of siliceous rocks found near the sea.

I am sure many individuals have had the opportunity to build sandcastles. Sandcastles are very easy to build and can easily be washed away by the sea. It does not take much effort or depth to build on sand. Likewise, superficial and shallow relationships will suffer when the storms of life come and the floods hit. The *sand* is easily washed away and all that is standing on it.

When our lives are aligned with God's word then we can stand on the rock of His word because it is solid, and it is truth and relevant for our lives today. When we are faced with challenges, like Moses, He gives us the assurance we need because He is the one that is with us and works through us. He just needs us to co-operate with Him so that the assignment can be fulfilled. My friend has a saying: *We are His hands and feet.* Just like God used Moses to demonstrate His power and authority to the ruling Egyptian Empire, He seeks individuals who are willing to fulfill His assignments.

I did not realise it at the time, but my husband and I were digging a deep foundation before we were married. God dealt with numerous issues in both of our lives. He surrounded me with people who helped, advised and supported me on my journey as He healed me and helped me to grow as a person. We have been married now for twenty-seven years and have two wonderful sons. I cannot believe how quickly the time has passed.

I sometimes reflect on how life might have been had I still harboured unresolved issues prior to being married. The healing process brought laughter, tears, hurt and pain. It was difficult sometimes, but on reflection, it was all worth it. The whole process prepared me and enabled me to be the person that I am today, whole and balanced, focused and dependent on God my Creator. I also have a deep settled peace which goes beyond all understanding. The process prepared me to be a wife, mother, an employee, an entrepreneur, a Sunday school teacher and to be involved in other ministerial duties at my local church. I am by no means perfect and I still have a lot to learn but I can relate to this statement from:

1 Timothy 6:6 (KJV)

*But godliness with contentment is great gain. For we brought nothing into this world, and it is certain we can carry nothing out.*

Godliness in this context equates to holiness, which is a word that is not used very often today. It means to have reverence towards God, to show great respect towards Him and His laws. Jesus Christ demonstrated this when He was alive on earth and that is why God said that He was pleased with Him. We too can emanate this life when Christ is at the centre of our life and we allow Him to be in the driving seat of our life so He too can teach us. It is about knowing that God is so special in your life and that you love Him for who He is.

It is also about knowing He has a purpose and a plan for you. It is about understanding that whatever you have, has been entrusted to you by God. Therefore, you are not the owner of it, but you are looking after it on His behalf. It is about having the mindset of asking *How can I be a blessing to someone else with the possessions, gifts or talents God has entrusted to me?*

There are many ways in which we can bless other people. It may be a financial blessing or may be giving someone a lift to their destination, it may be helping them with something, it may be feeding the homeless, giving a word of encouragement, praying for them or sharing some information with them. It is about having the heart and wisdom of wanting to share. It is about understanding stewardship.

There is an individual in the Bible who did not understand this concept. His name is Nabal and we can see what happened as a consequence of his actions in 1 Samuel 25.

Nabal was a very rich man who had many possessions including three thousand sheep and one thousand goats. He had a beautiful and understanding wife called Abigail. However Nabal was described as being rude and mean spirited. Now David, who was anointed to be the future king of Israel, was being pursued by the reigning king, Saul, whom I look at in more detail later. King Saul was jealous and felt threatened by the fact that David was going to be his successor and not his own son. In order to ensure his dynasty, Saul made it his assignment to kill David and literally pursued him as a lion pursues its prey.

Consequently, David was living as a fugitive in the wilderness with some of his soldiers. One day David heard that Nabal's shepherds were shearing some of his sheep. His soldiers were to inform Nabal that they had formed an affinity with his shepherds and had not taken advantage of them and in fact had protected them whilst they were caring for his sheep. Therefore, they were to ask Nabal if he could spare some food for them. Nabal's response was disproportionate to the request and was arrogant and venomous.

1 Samuel 25:10–11

> ...Who does this son (David) of Jesse think he is? There are lots of servants these days who run away from their masters.
>
> Should I take my bread and my water and my meat that I've slaughtered for my shearers and give it to a gang who comes from God knows where?

That was Nabal's response to the future king. And probably would have been his response to anyone else who asked for assistance. Quite simply, Nabal could have just said, No.

The Bible reminds us in Ecclesiastes 5:3 (KJV)

> ...; and a fool's voice is known by multitude of words.

Nabal said too much and clearly infuriated David. He also did not understand the concept of stewardship and referred to what he had as *my* bread, *my* water and *my* meat. He did not understand that he was extremely blessed, and part of his assignment was to be a blessing to others in need. He clearly had resources that were in abundance of what he needed for himself, his family and his employees. He did not comprehend that his position of power and wealth was not just for his benefit but that he was there to be an instrument whom God could use to help others who were less fortunate than himself.

Unfortunately, many people have that attitude of selfishness today and as a result do not experience the joy, peace and blessing of helping others. God wants to use us to demonstrate His power by being a blessing to others.

Acts 20:35 (KJV)

> ...It is more blessed to give than to receive.

As a result of Nabal's response, David became very angry and wanted revenge. Sometimes if we feel we have been treated unjustly we want to take matters into our own hands and *deal with the problem*. That was David's mindset at the time; he was intent on destroying Nabal because of his response. As previously stated, the book of Proverbs is a very practical book and has much to say about issues that are applicable to life today. It talks about the many emotions that we will experience in life and in this case, has much to say about anger.

Proverbs 15:18

> *A quick tempered man starts fights; a cool-tempered man tries to stop them.*

Proverbs 14:29

> *A wise man controls his temper. He knows that anger causes mistakes.*

My husband has often said to me, "Do not make decisions when you are angry as you usually regret them." I know from my experience as a parent that this is true. Anger is a very powerful emotion that can corrupt our thinking, cloud our judgment and affect our actions. That is why the Bible warns against it. This needs to be balanced with the fact that there will be times in our lives where we will become angry or we will be upset by someone's words or actions towards us but once again we have the power to choose our response.

Ephesians 4:26 (KJV)

*Be ye angry, and sin not: let not the sun go down upon your wrath: Neither give place to the devil.*

Here we are being reminded to choose not to sin whilst experiencing the emotion of anger. We have the power to choose to be in control of our attitudes, responses and actions. If we choose not to exercise self-control, then we are consciously or unconsciously allowing the perpetrator to *press our buttons* like a remote control in order for us to react. Thus, they then have the power of influence over our emotions and actions.

Proverbs 25:28

*A man without self-control is as a defenceless city with broken down walls.*

Imagine an army going into battle finding out that the city about to be attacked has no walls or defenses. It would make the attack quite easy and the city itself would be extremely vulnerable. That is what happens when one is not able to demonstrate self-control. You are left defenseless, vulnerable and exposed to external forces.

David had clearly *lost it*. You can feel how incensed he was by what Nabal had said. He had left himself wide open to his feelings of anger and injustice as a result of the public comments made by Nabal.

1 Samuel 25:21–22

*David had been saying to himself, "A lot of good it did us to help this fellow. We protected his flocks in the wilderness so that not one thing was lost or stolen, but he has repaid me bad for good. All that I get for my trouble is insults.*

*May God curse me if even one of his men remains alive by tomorrow morning."*

Fortunately, one of Nabal's shepherds informed Abigail what Nabal had said. He confirmed that David and his men had been very protective and friendly towards them.

Abigail being an understanding woman was able to exercise wisdom, knowledge, prudence and discretion. She was an intelligent woman who clearly operated in alignment with the word of God.

Proverbs 15:1–2 (KJV)

*A soft answer turneth away wrath: but grievous words stir up anger.*

*The tongue of the wise useth knowledge aright: but the mouth of fools poureth out foolishness.*

Proverbs 15: 4

*Gentle words cause life and health; griping brings discouragement.*


Abigail acknowledged the graveness of the situation and quickly recognised the importance of reconciliation, compassion and care. She quickly prepared a great deal of food for David and his men but did not tell Nabal. When she approached David, she showed humility and responded to him accordingly.


1 Samuel 25:24–25

*"I accept all blame in this matter, my lord," she said. "Please listen to what I want to say.*

*Nabal is a bad-tempered boor, but please don't pay any attention to what he said. He is a fool—just like his name means. But I didn't see the messengers you sent."*


Abigail was successful in diffusing the anger that David had exerted and was able to save him from making a decision that he probably would have regretted. She demonstrated courage as she knew that David was extremely angry, but she still stepped out in the face of adversity not knowing what the outcome was going to be. She demonstrated amazing negotiation and management skills by quickly obtaining food for the men and sending her servant ahead and then having a gracious dialogue with David. She managed to save her household due to her wisdom. Abigail was clearly aligned with God's word as can be seen by her interactions with David. She was able to complete the assignment as she diffused the *ticking time bomb* that could have exploded and brought destruction not only to her, but her family, employees and David himself. David commended Abigail as his response to her intervention was:

1 Samuel 25: 32–34

> *David replied to Abigail, "Bless the Lord God of Israel who has sent you to meet me today.*
>
> *Thank God for your good sense. Bless you for keeping me from murdering the man and carrying out vengeance with my own hands.*
>
> *For I swear by the Lord, the God of Israel who has kept me from hurting you, that if you had not come out to meet me, not one of Nabal's men would be alive tomorrow morning."*

When Abigail returned home, she discovered that Nabal had arranged a party that was fit for a king. He was described to be merry and very drunk (1 Samuel 25:36). It does not seem that Nabal ever felt any guilt or shame; knowing that someone had approached him for food which he could have easily spared but his response was so scornful. Subsequently after he had sobered up the following day, Abigail told him of her meeting with David. He ended up having a stroke and later died.

Imagine how differently the outcome might have been for Nabal if he applied the general principle of compassion and generosity. Nabal did not acknowledge that his blessings and resources were from God and he was only a steward of them. He clearly rejected his assignment, but God found someone else that was willing to take on the assignment; Abigail.

Proverbs 11:17

*Your own soul is nourished when you are kind; it is destroyed when you are cruel.*

Proverbs 11:24–25

*It is possible to give away and become richer. It is also possible to hold too tightly and lose everything.*

*Yes the liberal man shall be rich. By watering others, he waters himself.*

I believe David would no doubt have remembered the kindness that was shown towards him by Nabal, if he had accepted the assignment appropriately. I also believe David would have rewarded him handsomely at some future stage in his life.

David was not a perfect person (as many of us are not) but he was a man who kept his word. This can be seen when he wanted to fulfill a promise, he had made to his best friend Jonathan (king Saul's son) many years before he himself became king. Even though Jonathan had died tragically in a battle, when David became king, he remembered the promise to never stop showing kindness to Jonathan's family. He sought out Jonathan's descendant and fulfilled the promise by allowing him to live in the palace and took care of him.

2 Samuel 9:1

*One day David began wondering if any of Saul's family was still living, for he wanted to be kind to them, as he had promised Prince Jonathan.*

The palace officials managed to find Mephibosheth who was the son of Jonathan. When he was brought into the presence of king David, he was clearly afraid but was later reassured.

2 Samuel 9:7

> *But David said, "Don't be afraid. I've asked you to come so that I can be kind to you because of my vow to your father Jonathan. I will restore to you all the land of your grandfather Saul, and you shall live here in the palace."*

There was another occasion where a friend of David who was also a king had died and David sent his condolences via his officials.

1 Chronicles 19:1–2

> *When King Nahash of Ammon died, his son Hanun became the new king. Then David declared, "I am going to show friendship to Hanun because of all the kind things his father did for me."*

I am not saying that Nabal should have helped David because he was going to be the future king. In that case it would have been a matter of *giving to receive*. I am stating that regardless of who had approached him, Nabal was in a position to help. It would not have impacted upon him financially or economically to have shared a little of what he had been blessed with. Nabal's attitude was off the mark and he was clearly out of alignment with God's word.

The opposite of contentment is greed. Many people are not contented in life. They are always seeking and striving for things that they think will make them happy. They are never satisfied or fulfilled and do not like to share what they have. This could be information that could help someone, finances or volunteering their time in some way. Other adjectives for such a person might be that they are identified as been mean or selfish. It doesn't matter what we accumulate in life, as my old Pastor used to say, *"I have never seen a removal van at a funeral."* Likewise, in the case of Nabal, when he passed away all his possessions were left behind.

There is so much that can be learnt from 1 Samuel 25; so many different characters, attitudes and challenges. The beautiful thing in this chapter is that God is able to use one person to change the trajectory of another person's life.

Therefore, we all have the ability to impact the life of others around us. Never think or believe that you are insignificant, unworthy or incapable of making an impact. If Abigail believed that, she would not have taken the action that she did. Our thoughts are very powerful and if we think we are insignificant then we will act accordingly. If we believe we can make an impact, then we will.

Proverbs 23:7 (KJV)

*For as he thinketh in his heart, so is he:*

The greatest gift that this world has ever received is the gift that was given by God Himself.

John 3:16 (KJV)

*For God so loved the world that he gave his only begotten Son, that whosoever believeth in him should not perish, but have everlasting life.*

With this is mind, how can we refuse to give out of the abundance of what God gives to us? He wants to use us to bless and meet the needs others. Therefore, it should be understood that it is actually a privilege to be able to be used by God to deliver a blessing.

## Little Me....

Little me...but who told you so?
Were you there when I thought of you, And how you'd grow?
I made you, you're mine,
Look inside you, I'm here.
Stop listening to the voices that tell you you're a tare.

There's nobody like me who can give sweet rest,
Stop looking around you
You are my very best
Out of all my creation, it's in you my image reflects.

So, come up high to where I abide
And behold your future from my own eyes.
It's one where I'll never leave,
and I'll stay by your side.

My child I love you and I want to see you thrive
To go forth and become the vision and the apple of mine eye.
Don't you fear what man may say,
Don't listen to the voice of the adversary.

Gird yourself up in the armour I've given you
Be strong and courageous, haven't I told you?
I will always be with you.

*H. Henry*

# Chapter Five

## Living in Alignment

Living in alignment releases one from bitterness and resentment.

There is a Jewish woman in the Bible called Naomi who had fallen upon hard times. Her life was turned upside down for a number of reasons. There was a famine in her town of Bethlehem. This caused the family to migrate to Moab. After migrating her two sons married Moabite women, then her husband died and then her two sons died.

All she had left were her two daughters-in-law Ruth and Orpah. Rather than remain in Moab, Naomi decided to return to her home town as she heard that the economic situation had improved there. On the way she advised her daughters-in-law to return to their parents as she felt she had nothing to offer them. It appears as though Naomi had a strong bond with her daughters-in-law as both of them wanted to remain with her, even in such dire circumstances.

Ruth 1:8-10

> *But after they had begun their homeward journey, she changed her mind and said to her two daughters-in-law, "Why don't you return to your parents" homes instead of coming with me? And may the Lord reward you for your faithfulness to your husbands and to me.*
>
> *And may he bless you with another happy marriage." Then she kissed them and they all broke down and cried.*

*"No," they said. "We want to go with you to your people."*

It is wonderful and refreshing to learn that there was such a positive relationship between them as this is not always reflected between in-laws. In some cases, such relationships are just about tolerated and not nurtured. Orpah decided to take the advice of her mother-in-law. There is no indication of bitterness or resentment between them as she kissed her mother in law and said goodbye and returned to her homeland.

Ruth on the other hand was content to remain with her mother-in-law. She decided to walk by faith and not by sight. She did not know what the outcome of her life was going to be if she remained with her mother-in-law but there was no doubt in her mind that she was going to remain with her.

Ruth 1:16-18

*But Ruth replied, "Don't make me leave you, for I want to go wherever you go, and to live wherever you live; your people, and your God shall be my God;*

*I want to die where you die and be buried there. May the Lord do terrible things to me if I allow anything but death to separate us."*

*And when Naomi saw that Ruth had made up her mind and could not be persuaded otherwise, she stopped urging her.*

What a powerful statement to make. You can almost feel the love and intensity of what Ruth was saying to her mother-in-law. Here we can see that Ruth demonstrated that she was a woman of commitment, tenacity, faithfulness, resilience, determination and true conviction with regards to her belief in the same God as Naomi. This is important because Ruth would have been identified as a Gentile (non-Jewish) woman. Yet she was willing to embrace the Jewish traditions, culture and beliefs even though she did not have to. Ruth was now free to return to her homeland where they worshipped other gods. Ruth however, had learnt the art of alignment which nullified resentment and she demonstrated this not only in her talk but also in her actions.

When Naomi returned to Bethlehem, Ruth set to work in the field to collect grain for herself and her mother-in-law. She placed herself in an environment where their needs could be met as they were in need of food. She did not sit down and wait for the food to be brought to her, she went out to collect it herself. At a time when they could have been depressed and feeling sorry for themselves, they were optimistic as they continued to believe in God.

In addition to the other attributes mentioned, Ruth was conscientious, focused and hopeful.

Ruth 2:2-3

> *One day Ruth said to Naomi, "Perhaps I can go out into the fields of some kind man to glean the free grain behind his reapers." And Naomi said, "Alright dear daughter. Go ahead."*
>
> *So she did. And as it happened, the field where she found herself belonged to Boaz, this relative of Naomi's husband.*

Ruth made the statement "*Perhaps I can go out into the fields of some kind man to glean the free grain behind his reapers.*" Out of all the fields that were available, Ruth was led to the field of a very *kind man*. This was not a coincidence. I believe this was God's incident as the field was also owned by a relative of Naomi's late husband. His name was Boaz, whom Ruth had probably never met before or even heard of as they previously lived in Moab.

The conclusion of the story is that Ruth gained a good reputation for her hard work, love and commitment towards her mother-in-law in the town.

Ruth 2:11-12

> ...Boaz replied, "and I also know about all the love and kindness you have shown your mother-in-law since the death of your husband, and how you left your father and mother in your own land and have come here to live among strangers.
>
> May the Lord God of Israel, under whose wings you have come to take refuge, bless you for it."

Ruth's actions caught the attention of the people in the town and God Almighty himself. She made it her assignment to love, care and provide for her mother-in-law, even though she was a widow herself. She was a foreigner in a strange land. She was single and had no form of regular income, yet she placed the needs of her mother-in-law above her own needs. Ruth had a servant's heart and as she aligned with God's word and His will, He provided their overall needs.

Deuteronomy 10:18

> He gives justice to the fatherless and widows. He loves foreigners and gives them food and clothing.

Due to a Jewish tradition, Ruth eventually married Boaz, who was a more mature and wealthy man, and she gave birth to a son. Not only was Ruth blessed, but Naomi was inevitably blessed too through the love and commitment Ruth showed to her.

Ruth 4:13-15

> *So Boaz married Ruth, and when he slept with her, the Lord gave her a son.*
>
> *And the women of the city said to Naomi, "Bless the Lord who has given you this little grandson; may he be famous in Israel.*
>
> *May he restore your youth and take care of you in your old age; for he is the son of your daughter-in-law who loves you so much, and who has been kinder to you than seven sons."*

The child that Ruth gave birth to was called Obed, who is the grandfather of king David. Naomi and Ruth suffered so much loss and grief that at times they probably could not even begin to imagine that their lives would eventually be entwined with wealth, security, stability and eventually, royalty. However, through the process of trust, contentment and living one day at a time in alignment with God and His word, God showed them favour and opened doors of opportunity in the midst of adversity in order to fulfill His plan and His purposes.

It is also interesting that king David seems to have inherited some of his great-grandmother and great-grandfather's attributes. David clearly loved God and there were occasions where he too had to show strength of character in very challenging situations. He too was focused, determined, resilient, displayed loyalty to king Saul and showed kindness to others.

When we have a relationship with Christ, He wants us to be in a state of contentment and not resentment regardless of the difficulties we are experiencing. However, this cannot be achieved if we choose to compromise the truth of His word and seek to blame others or justify ourselves without taking responsibility for what we choose to align ourselves with. We literally prevent God from acting on our behalf because He cannot be aligned with sin. Sometimes human nature has a tendency to compartmentalise sin or compare itself with other people and consequently comes to the conclusion, *Well I am not as bad as so and so, or everyone else is doing it, so why should it matter?* This is a very dangerous place to be. Instead of being aligned with God and His word, the alignment is being made with another flawed human being. God wants us and expects us to come to Him for help to be realigned. He wants to use us to fulfil his assignments so we too can be blessed and experience the contentment of being aligned with Him without bitterness or resentment.

Matthew 6:8 (KJV)

*...Remember, your Father knows exactly what you need even before you ask him*

Imagine having that kind of assurance in a relationship; someone knows what you *need* even before you ask. God was fully aware of Naomi's and Ruth's circumstances and therefore met their needs accordingly. Similarly, He is fully aware of our circumstances and needs but we still have to trust him as He knows what is best.

Philippians 4:19 (KJV)

*But my God will supply all your need according to his riches in glory by Christ Jesus.*

Armed with the knowledge that *God will supply all your needs,* makes the completion of assignments even easier. God is not asking us to do something He believes we cannot do. In other words, He is not setting us up to fail. *No.* God is setting us up to experience an abundant life that was promised to us. It is written in the word of God therefore, we can hold Him accountable as long as we are submitting to being in alignment with His will and His word.

I am not saying this process is likely to be a bed of roses or that it will be an easy journey. Naomi and Ruth demonstrated that we can experience some real hardship in life, but it is our response to God that will really determine the outcome of the event. Therefore, there is likely to be some cost in terms of sacrifice, faith, trust, emotional turmoil and maybe some pain, but anything worth having will come at some expense. We all know that if you have had to personally pay the price for something, you tend to value and appreciate it more.

The process of alignment in order to alleviate resentment might be to address something that God has brought to your attention that has been bothering you for years. It might also be to get some help with an issue. It might be to pursue that dream you have always had instead of being resentful of someone else's success. It might be to repent of something that you are doing that is clearly out of alignment with God and His word and come back into alignment with Him.

You choose whether to exist in your current state or to seek God and ask Him to help you deal with whatever it is He has revealed to you. Will you be obedient and respond accordingly? If Naomi and Ruth decided to remain in Moab in a state of bitterness and resentfulness, they would not have met Boaz and their lives would not have been recorded in history. Life becomes so much more meaningful and content when you respond to God's call upon your life and seek to remain in alignment with Him.

Moses, Elijah, king Jehoshaphat, king George VI, the British Nation, Ruth, Naomi, myself and many others have taken steps of faith to begin a journey and as my friend would say, *"Not knowing what the end of the journey is going to look like but until you make that step you will never know."*

I close this chapter by sharing a couple of stories. Firstly, after many years my husband was ready for a change at work. He subsequently applied for another job. He told a work colleague about the job he was going to apply for and asked if he would give him a reference. Of course, his colleague agreed but then decided to apply for the job himself as he was more experienced in that particular field than my husband. He was successful and got the job.

My husband aligned himself with the word of God. He did not show any bitterness or resentment and in fact, was happy for his colleague. He knew that God was in the driving seat of his life and that whatever happened was according to God's will.

Romans 8:28 (KJV)

*And we know that all things work together for the good to them that love God, to them who are the called according to His purpose.*

I know other individuals who would have responded differently but as my husband has always stated, "You choose your response." A few weeks later there was another vacancy at the same office. My husband decided to apply for that job too. Once again, he was unsuccessful, and my husband was disappointed but was happy for his other colleague who was successful. It seemed that everyone else was *abandoning ship* and he was being left behind.

God, however, had another plan. Many people had become disillusioned at my husband's workplace, that is why they wanted to leave. In order to try to retain the staff there was an incentive whereby there would be a gradual but significant increase in their salaries. Consequently, the successful candidate that had agreed to give my husband a reference decided to stay put, although he did not communicate this to my husband.

A few days later my husband received a phone call from the manager who had initially interviewed him for the job. My husband was unavailable and so he left him a message. My husband was not keen to return the call immediately, but I encouraged him to do so. It transpired that the manager became aware that the other candidate was going to remain in his current position and he now wanted my husband to join their team.

At the time when my husband applied for the job the pay incentive was not due to be implemented. However, when the manager asked him to join his team, it had been implemented. Subsequently, my husband said that he would join the team, if they would match his new salary. They agreed. Therefore, he got a pay rise and a new job and was and still is, very happy.

My husband could have given up at any stage and allowed the rejection and betrayal of his colleague to consume him, but he didn't. He could have been very negative towards his colleague, but he wasn't. God was on the job and He was in the driving seat all along. My husband took some steps not knowing what the outcome was going to be and even though it seemed like he was being *left behind,* God was working on a plan that benefitted my husband and our family. That is what can happen when you allow God to be in the driving seat. When you are willing to come into alignment you have the added benefit of contentment that God will work things out in your favour.

The second story is from an occasion when I was in need of a new vehicle. I was looking for a vehicle that was similar to the one I had previously owned. I wanted an upgrade on certain specifications such as leather seats, one previous owner, low mileage, full-service history and good condition. I was constantly checking AutoTrader® and Gumtree® online. I was so desperate to find something that I allowed the matter to consume me for a few weeks.

My husband said to me one day *"Just give it a break and stop looking."* At first, I thought it was bad advice as I did not want to miss out on finding a vehicle but then I decided to take his advice and stopped looking.

I commenced the search again a few days later. I saw a vehicle that matched the specifications I wanted. I called the owner, who duly informed me that someone else had arranged to see the vehicle. I was so desperate that I asked him if I was able to see the vehicle first, would he let me have the first refusal. He said, *"No"* and that he was a man of his word. He had already promised that the other person could see the vehicle first. I was disappointed but then a sense of guilt came over me as I realised that I was trying to persuade someone to be dishonourable to satisfy my own need and not trusting God to meet my need. I knew I was wrong and prayed about it and asked for forgiveness. It was at that point that I came into alignment with God's word as I had been convicted by the Holy Spirit.

At that point, the anxiety and desperation of wanting to find a vehicle left and I began to trust God. I was no longer consumed with spending all my time and energy looking for a vehicle and inevitably became less stressed.

As I became more relaxed, I leisurely checked *Gumtree®* and *Autotrader®* and then, one day, I saw a vehicle that had just been posted on Gumtree. It met every specification that I required. I phoned the gentleman and he stated that someone had offered to buy the vehicle without seeing it, but he had refused the offer. I was the first person that actually wanted to see it but I could not get there until the following day as he was some distance away. Despite this he said he would not let anyone else see the vehicle and that he would give me the first refusal.

When I arrived and saw the vehicle, I could barely contain my excitement. It was exactly what I had been looking for and in fact was beyond my expectations. The body work was immaculate; it had a low mileage, one previous owner, full- service history, leather seats and a clean interior. I purchased the vehicle without hesitation as I knew God had provided it for me. After I purchased the vehicle the gentleman asked me how far I had to travel to get back home. I told him and he said, *"Follow me to the petrol station."* I followed him and after the vehicle was filled with fuel, he went and paid the bill. That is the God we serve and that is how He wants to operate in our lives. If we are willing to stand aside and let Him have His way, as we come into alignment with Him and His word. God does not need our help, but He does require our cooperation by surrendering our will to His.

Philippians 4:6–7

*Don't worry about anything; instead, pray about everything; tell God your needs, and don't forget to thank him for his answers.*

*If you do this, you will experience God's peace, which is far more wonderful than the human mind can understand. His peace will keep your thoughts and your hearts quiet and at rest as you trust in Christ Jesus.*

Being able to apply that Scripture to every aspect of your life brings true contentment.

## Do you Remember?

*Do you remember the times we once had?*
*Morning and night these days made me glad.*
*A solace in you my sweet hiding place,*
*The warmth of your love, your tender embrace.*

*My longing for you from the depths of my soul*
*A simple touch is all it takes to make me whole.*
*Restoration is when I align myself with you*
*It's time to take back what was stolen and wrongly used.*

*Do you remember…. Of course, I do.*
*No time to look back and ponder*
*Pick up your cross, for the latter rain will be greater,*
*Fight on and be strong*
*And watch me perform wonders.*

**H. Henry**

# Chapter Six

## You Choose what You Accomplish

According to the Oxford Dictionary, accomplish means to achieve or complete successfully. (www.oxfordlearnersdictionaries.com web.27 May 2020)

When we arrive in this world, we have all been given gifts, talents, time and resources. You choose what you do with what you have been given. A friend of mine once said, *"If it's going to be, it's up to me."* I like that because it is true. The responsibility clearly lies with you. You decide what you will do with what you have been given.

There are many resources available to assist you on the journey. As I have previously said, you probably just need to take the first step and you will be surprised how things start to come together and doors start to open.

I once heard a story about a teacher who told a child to sit down in his classroom. He did not want to, but he eventually sat down. He then said to the teacher, *"I may be sitting down...but I am still standing up inside."* That is the power of the will and the power of choice. It is not only what you want people to see externally but also about what is going on inside of your mind and once again, it all comes back to choosing what you want to align with.

Whatever you choose to align yourself with, will determine what you will become and what you will accomplish in your life. I have already discussed what it means to come into alignment with God's word and His perspective of you. It is up to you whether you accept and believe what He sees and what He has given you. I recently heard someone quote Hans Urs von Balthasar on the radio. *What you are is God's gift to you, what you become is your gift to God.* That is such a profound and powerful statement.

I watched a movie a few years ago called Gifted Hands. It is a story based on true events about a child who came from a broken home and deprived background. His mother was illiterate, and the child was labelled as being the *dumbest child in the whole world* by the other class members. Unfortunately, his grades reflected this, as in one school test, he actually obtained zero.

He was destined to become another statistic who probably would have become involved in a life of crime and gang culture in order to survive. His mother worked as a cleaner for a professor and as she was cleaning his study, she was amazed at the number of books he had and asked him if he had read all of them. He said, *"Yes."*

That was a *light bulb moment* for her. She believed in her children and she also believed in God. She prayed for wisdom on how to help her children strive for a better life and for them to obtain a good education. She prayed about the situation and put into practice what she believed God had told her. She told her two sons they were going to be restricted on the amount of television they watched in the week. She also said they were going to go to the library and read two books per week on any subject they chose. They had to write an assignment on what they had learnt and share the information with her. This was separate from any homework they had to do.

It seemed like a tall mountain to climb at the time, but the children accepted the challenge.

Whilst going through puberty, there had been a time when the author became very defiant and presented extremely challenging behaviour both at home and at school. He almost became involved in a life of crime and violence as he became angry and lost his temper one day at school and sought to attack one of his peers.

He realised he had serious anger issues and that caused him to cry out to God. He asked Jesus Christ to help him. His prayer was answered and his life began to change. He began to excel in his education and his confidence increased. Teachers began to see the change in his attitude and his desire to learn, so much so that they went above and beyond to help him achieve his dreams and ambitions. In a nutshell, the doors began to open, and opportunities came his way.

To cut a long story short, this child grew up to become a world-renowned neurosurgeon. His name is Dr Ben Carson. I encourage you to watch the movie, *Gifted Hands,* and read his books. They are such an encouragement and inspiration of how he succeeded with God's help against all odds. He overcame racial discrimination, poverty, inequality and deprivation. He had a paradigm shift that resulted in him not accepting the negatives of what others believed about him. By coming into alignment with what his mother asked of him and recognising that God had a plan for his life, he was able to accomplish great things and impacted the world around him. Dr Carson accomplished his ambition and when you read his books and or watch the film, you will see that it was not an easy journey, but the reality is, he never gave up.

Imagine if he did not come into alignment with what his mother had asked. Imagine if he was a rebellious teenager who said, *"No way, I'm not going to do that."* Imagine if Dr Carson had not cried out to his Creator when he hit those challenging *potholes* in his life, he would never have accomplished the great things that he has.

This world would have been robbed of one of the best neurosurgeons that ever lived. He was one of the first neurosurgeons to undertake operations involving twins conjoined at the head where both survived after being separated. He used his gifts and talents along with his motivation and desires to change the outcome of his life and others. This is just one individual. Imagine if we all tapped into our untouched potential and aligned ourselves with God and His word. I guarantee this world would be a different place.

There was a time in my life when I became dissatisfied with my job. I felt like I needed a new challenge and subsequently applied for a job to become a social worker in the Isles of Jersey. I really wanted the job as Jersey is a beautiful place with over twenty beaches. I was successful in my application and was offered the job. My husband had completed his degree two years before and had received a promotion. I tried to persuade him (and myself) that it would be a good move for the whole family. He was not interested, as the contract on offer was only for five years and he said it would be irresponsible to give up job security for a five-year contract. Our two sons were aged seven and two at the time.

I understood what my husband was saying but I was still torn as it was a new job with new opportunities. My husband said the decision was mine and if I wanted to go I could. He stated that he would not stand in my way, but he would remain in the UK. I know not everyone would have been given this option by their spouse, but my husband later said he wanted me to make the decision without his influence.

I thought long and hard about the job and even considered the possibility of commuting by air as the flight would only take an hour. I then thought about living there part-time and spending the rest of my time in the UK. When I weighed up all the options, I decided not to accept the job.

We laugh about it now and when the topic comes up my husband often says, *"I would never have applied for that job and would not even think to leave my family."* In all honesty, I would not have left them either, but I was still disappointed.

As a result, I said to myself I would never apply for another job as I did not want to put myself in that position again. I decided there and then that if I was going to change my job, I would work for myself and have my own business. Consequently, I stopped looking for a new job.

A few months later we had a visitor from abroad whom we had known for a number of years. He told us that he wanted to share some information with us he had never shared with us before. He told us he was involved in buying and renting properties. On reflection, God had sent him on an assignment to us to share that information as it was like music to our ears. My husband and I had discussed wanting to become involved with property many years before, but we did not know the process of how to turn the dream into reality.

Our friend coached us from beginning to end and even attended a seminar with us whilst he was here on holiday. The seminar facilitators went on to promote a course that was in the region of three thousand pounds for more detailed information. We did not have that kind of money and our friend said he had been on a similar course and had all the books and resources at home. He promised that once he got home, he would send us all the materials he had and we could keep them as long as necessary.

We had known our friend for years, but he never shared the information about his property portfolio before. If he had, it probably would have sounded like a great story at the time but would not have had the same impact. On reflection it brought light into a dark situation and he had no idea what I had said previously and how disgruntled I was feeling at work but that is how God works as He knows everything.

The information he had provided was the catalyst we needed to jump start our aspiration for becoming involved with property. It was amazing. Just after I read all the materials another friend at work who I did not know was also involved in property, shared some vital information and literally showed me a property she had purchased and renovated and was now renting out.

When you begin to align yourself with God's word and His purpose, it is amazing how doors begin to open, and resources and information tend to flow in your direction. I do not call this a coincidence. Again I call it a *God incident*. It was not long before I gleaned further information from other family members and friends and some years later, I found myself working for myself. Applying for the job in Jersey still played a role as it helped me to focus on my goals. Had I not applied for the job, I probably would not have explored other opportunities. I am truly thankful for God's intervention in my situation as it changed my future and allowed me to try something new. I have learnt so much along the way about myself that I probably would never have known had I remained where I was. Many of the skills that I had developed whilst employed, I have been able to transfer to my new ventures; so once again, nothing was wasted.

We worked hard and accomplished our dream and then helped others to accomplish theirs by giving advice and support. Many years later, individuals have come back to me and thanked me, but I in turn, thank God.

I hope you can see how being in alignment, fulfilling your assignment and accomplishing God's will all work together in harmony. It is also amazing because those who are in close proximity to you inevitably benefit from the overspill of the blessing, just like Naomi did with Ruth. When you know who you are in Christ and He is the centre of your life, His will propels you to help others. This can then enable others to come into alignment so they too can fulfil their assignment and accomplish great things for God.

Jesus Christ knew who He was: the son of God. He knew what His purpose was: to die on the cross and become the sacrifice for our sin. While He knew that was the objective, it did not stop him from associating and accomplishing great things and impacting the lives of a variety of individuals who were in need of His help. He healed the sick, forgave those who had done wrong, set people free from oppression and taught many principles about God's kingdom while He was waiting to fulfill his main objective.

Luke 4:18–19

> ...the Spirit of the Lord is upon me; he has appointed me to preach Good News to the poor; he has sent me to heal the broken hearted and to announce that captives shall be released and the blind shall see, that the downtrodden shall be freed from their oppressors, and that God is ready to give blessings to all who come to him.

Jesus also impacted the lives of those who were closest to him, namely His disciples. They too, continued in the ministry of preaching and teaching the Gospel of Jesus Christ. Lives are still being impacted and changed through this Gospel over two thousand years later.

There were also occasions when Jesus was challenged by the religious and political leaders of the day.

Matthew 27:40 (KJV)

> ...If thou be the Son of God, come down from the cross.

Matthew 27:13-14

> "Don't you hear what they are saying" Pilate demanded?

*But Jesus said nothing, much to the governor's surprise.*


Despite the numerous challenges Jesus faced, He did not have to prove who He was for people to believe Him.

Likewise, you too will face challenges in your life and people will question you, but don't let that stop you from being in alignment with God's word. Look at the impact Jesus made on the people He served. There are many others who impacted the lives of others including Moses, Joshua, David, Ruth, Naomi, Abigail and many other patriarchs in the Bible.

Although alignment means to come into line, it also has a rippling effect. When a pebble is thrown into water it forms ripples that continue well after the stone has sunk and accentuates out as the ripples increase in size. As we come into alignment great things are being accomplished and we may never know how we have impacted someone else's life but in reality, it does not matter. What matters is that we fulfill our assignment.

When we were married, my husband and I did not have a television for about two years and it was lovely. We spent time talking, reading, studying and praying together and although we both worked full-time, we had some great quality time together. This all helped to build a solid foundation for our marriage. On reflection, I really thank God that He helped me to begin the process of alignment with His word and address some issues before we were married, otherwise I know for a fact I would have brought *baggage* into the marriage including insecurity, low self-esteem, lack of trust and lack of confidence. Once married, I continued to come into alignment with the truth of God's word (it is an ongoing process). I soon learned that I could not expect my husband to meet my every need and insecurities, after all he is only human. Without these issues being resolved, I know I would have constantly blamed myself if and when problems arose and internalised all that guilt, hurt and pain on top of the hurt and pain that was already there. While writing this I cannot help but think I would have been a very needy person; in need of constant reassurance, and that would have been emotionally exhausting for anyone. There would have come a point where the well of sympathy and patience from my husband would have dried up or the emotional bank account would have been overdrawn and ... you can guess what the outcome would have been.

I am not saying that after twenty-seven years of marriage we have not had our challenges, but when we have issues, we first look and see if we are in alignment with God's word. If not, then we do something about it and not just ignore it because as Christians, we believe that God's word is the final authority. Thus, He has enabled us to work through our issues together as a team, and to support each other.

God speaks to us through His written word and the book of Nehemiah illustrates how God positioned Nehemiah to accomplish an assignment. Nehemiah lived at a time when the Persian Empire dominated the world. He was originally from Jerusalem but was now living in exile. He worked for the king of Persia as a cup bearer (which means he tasted the king's wine before the king in order to protect the king from being poisoned by his enemies). Nehemiah was visited by some people from his hometown, Jerusalem. He asked how the residents of Jerusalem were and about the city of Jerusalem. They reported that the walls of Jerusalem were broken down and the gates were burnt down (in those days people lived in walled cities). Therefore, the city of Jerusalem was left exposed and open to attack from enemies.

This made Nehemiah very sad and depressed. He began to mourn and cry and decided to fast and pray. He cried out to God and reminded God of His promises. He came into alignment with God's word as he approached God in prayer. He humbled himself and recognised that the nation of Israel had chosen to disobey God's commandments and they were now suffering the consequences of their actions. He cried out to God to forgive them.

During this time the king observed that Nehemiah was not his usual self and was of a sad disposition. He asked him what was wrong, and Nehemiah was afraid to answer as he was not sure how the king would react to his response. Despite this, Nehemiah was honest and said he was sad because Jerusalem, the land of his ancestors was in ruins. Then the king asked him what he could do to help.

Before Nehemiah answered, he prayed and then asked the king if he could go to Judah to help rebuild Jerusalem. Nehemiah made himself available to take on the assignment to rebuild the walls of Jerusalem. He asked the king to provide him with official documents so that he could travel to Judah without any problems. He also asked if he could have some timber from the king's forests to make some beams and gates for the walls of Jerusalem. All of his requests were granted.

This assignment was for Nehemiah as God had positioned him to be in close proximity to the king, so much so that the king was sensitive to the change in his countenance. The king was interested in Nehemiah's well-being and wanted to help him. Therefore, God allowed Nehemiah to have access to the king's resources to enable him to complete the assignment. Nehemiah was also given protection by the king as he allowed him to travel with king's horsemen and captains.

The word of God reminds us that we too are protected when we are about the Lords business.


Psalms 34:7 (KJV)

*The angel of the LORD encampeth round them that fear him, and delivereth them.*

God had placed this assignment in Nehemiah's heart. It probably felt like a burden that he could not shake off as he felt the weight of it. Even when he arrived in Jerusalem, he did not reveal his purpose for being there until he had surveyed the land for himself and made an assessment of the situation. The assignment was incubated within Nehemiah until the time and conditions were right for it to be revealed as can be seen in the following verses.

Nehemiah 2:11 and 16–18

> *Three days after my arrival in Jerusalem I stole out during the night, taking only a few men with me; for I hadn't told a soul about the plans for Jerusalem which God had put into my heart….*
>
> *The city officials did not know I had been out there, or why, for as yet I had said nothing to anyone about my plans – not to the political or religious leaders, or even to those who would be doing the work.*
>
> *But now I told them "You know full well the tragedy of our city; it lies in ruins and its gates are burned. Let us rebuild the wall of Jerusalem and rid ourselves of this disgrace."*
>
> *Then I told them about the desire God had put into my heart, and of my conversation with the king, and the plan he had agreed. They replied at once, "Good. Let's rebuild the wall." And so, the work began.*

The accomplishment of the assignment did not come without opposition. There were some individuals who clearly sought to intimidate, manipulate and sabotage the overall work that was being accomplished. During those challenging times Nehemiah knew who had placed the assignment within his heart and so he went back to the assignor (God). He knew that as he was in alignment with God's plans, God had a responsibility to enable and empower him to fulfill the assignment. Therefore, when negative comments and threats were being made this was Nehemiah's response:

Nehemiah 4:4–5

*Then I prayed, "Hear us, O Lord God, for we are being mocked. May their scoffing fall back on their own heads and may they themselves become captives in a foreign land.*

*Do not ignore their sin. Do not blot it out, for they have despised you in despising us who are building your wall."*

Nehemiah did not become consumed or distracted by the opposition. He put the onus back on God and asked Him to deal with issues beyond his control namely, his enemies. Nehemiah dealt with the issues that were within his control. He ensured that the people continued to build but he also ensured they were able to protect themselves should they came under attack. They worked day and night. Half of the men built whilst the other half stood guard. The wall was finally built, and the city gates were erected. It was amazing that this vast task took only fifty-two days. The city of Jerusalem was now safe and secure.

The next task was for the city to be inhabited so that it could be a home that was maintained and protected for those who wished to return from exile. Nehemiah was very selective about who the inhabitants should be as they were surrounded by many enemies and he did not want them to infiltrate the city or lead the people into rebellion against God. A census was taken to try and prevent this from happening. The people had to prove their genealogy before they could occupy Jerusalem. As many of the families had come out of exile, they also had to rebuild their culture, traditions and come back into alignment with the commandments of God.

It cannot be taken for granted that Nehemiah was a great strategist, organiser and manager. He took his responsibilities seriously and it is clear that he did not have the mindset of starting something that he could not finish. He knew what his purpose was and although he did not know what the response was going to be from the king when he explained why he was feeling sad, he was open and honest. He even went further and asked the king to supply the timber that he needed to help with the rebuild. He believed in what he was called to do.

Throughout the book of Nehemiah, you get a sense of his personality; he cared for the well-being of the people. His role was not only to rebuild the walls of Jerusalem, but he was also rebuilding the confidence, values and the identity of the Jewish people. He reminded them of their great heritage, culture and the God they were called to serve, which he did not want to see lost again.

He was a man that was not easily intimidated and stood up to those who tried to forfeit the project. He was a discerning man who did not look at things at face value but looked at the motives of others. Therefore, he did not succumb to the tricks of his enemies. He was also a determined character who was able to encourage and motivate others into getting the job done.

You can see why God chose Nehemiah for this assignment. With the combination of his personality coupled with his gifts, talents and experiences, he was able to impact the lives of others around him. He willingly aligned himself and accepted the assignment God had placed in his heart and successfully accomplished the tasks not only rebuilding the walls of Jerusalem but also rebuilding the people and realigning them into fulfilling Gods purposes and plans. Once again, the mission was successfully accomplished as Nehemiah was committed to the task.

# Quiet

*Quiet you've instructed me to be*
*But what does it mean to wait upon thee?*

*Sitting at your feet observing your scarred hands*
*And seeing what you've endured in the place of man.*
*As I gaze deeper yet,*
*I see the beads of your weary sweat.*
*Father, I hear ... let this cup pass.*
*But not an echo came from Father, arrrh...alas*

*For this purpose, you came to set man free*
*So, we could be reunited to Father through thee.*

**H. Henry**

# Chapter Seven

## Little by Little, God will Give you what's Yours

My husband and I decided to relocate a few years after the birth of our first son as we wanted to be nearer to family. We spent a lot of time house hunting and checking out schools as our son was due to start primary school. Previously we had lived in a three-bed semi-detached house for about nine years that had not appreciated in value. Whilst house hunting, we saw a lovely house that was detached with four large bedrooms, a balcony off one of the bedrooms, two full size bathrooms, a study area, large kitchen diner, a separate lounge and dining room and a small rear garden.

The couple that was selling the house had retired and were now *living their dream* on a boat. I could see that they were keen to sell. As I looked around the house, I was overwhelmed thinking, *Could we really afford this?* Then the thought came, *this house is like a hotel you don't deserve it.* I remember coming away from that house with that thought in my mind also feeling fearful of the potential responsibility of taking on a house of that size and a mortgage to match. We did some research regarding the schools in the area and decided not to purchase it.

I share that story because sometimes we can be overwhelmed with that which God wants to bless us and therefore, become uncooperative. Subsequently we then talk ourselves out of what God wants to give us through fear and unbelief and forget what He has promised us.

It is so important that we have the capacity to absorb the blessings of the Lord. We have to be prepared spiritually and emotionally to receive whatever it is He has for us. If not, it is so easy for doubt and unbelief to paralyse us and consequently, we miss out on what God has in store for us.

This is demonstrated in Exodus 23 where the children of Israel are reminded of a promise God gave them regarding inheriting land. God promised that He would prepare the way for them and drive out the current inhabitants.

Exodus 23:29

*I will not do it all in one year, for the land would become a wilderness, and the wild animals would become too many to control.*

*But I will drive them out a little at a time, until your population has increased enough to fill the land.*

It is wonderful to know that God was telling the people that He would fulfill his promise in due time. God even disclosed His strategy as to how this would happen. It would be fulfilled in a way that was sustainable and manageable for them. He was not going to give them all the land He had promised all at once because they were not developed enough as a nation to inhabit it or manage it.

For those who love gardening, it is amazing to see that if a garden has not been tendered to for a few months it becomes overtaken with thorns, thistles, weeds and unwanted creatures. It takes time and energy for the garden to be returned to a state where it looks like a garden again.

I cannot think of anything in life that does not require some kind of maintenance be it a house, car, children, adults, plants or our bodies. God cared for the Israelites so much that He did not want them to be overwhelmed with the vast uninhabited land. Consequently, He promised that they would inherit the land in manageable segments.

This strategy can also be applied to us as His children. He knows that we can become overwhelmed with some things He wants to give us. He also knows whether we will be able to manage it well or not. Some of the reasons for poor management might be the lack of experience, lack of faith, disobedience or just the wrong timing for example.

Luke 16:10–12

> ...For unless you are honest in small matters, you won't be in large ones. If you cheat even a little, you won't be honest with greater responsibilities.
>
> And if you are untrustworthy about worldly wealth, who will trust you with the true riches of heaven?

Basically, we are being reminded that he who is faithful in little is faithful in much. In order for that to happen, we need to have the capacity to absorb what God has in store for us, or have the capacity to receive the blessings He wants to give to us. Therefore, if God wants to develop a certain area of our lives, He will allow us to face challenges to enable us to respond to them. Hopefully we will learn and grow from these challenges so that we develop the capacity to receive more of what He wants to give us.

God told Moses to send twelve spies into the land of Canaan to assess the land, which he had promised to give them.

Numbers 13: 27–29

*This was their report: "We arrived in the land you sent us to see, and it is indeed a magnificent country - a land "flowing with milk and honey." Here is some fruit we have brought as proof.*

*But the people living there are powerful, and their cities are fortified and very large; and what's more, we saw Anakim giants there."*

However, two out of the twelve spies had a different perspective.

Numbers 13:30–32

*But Caleb reassured the people as they stood before Moses. "Let us go up at once and possess it," he said, "for we are well able to conquer it."*

*"Not against people as strong as they are" the other spies said, "They would crush us."*

*So, the majority report of the spies was negative: the land is full of warriors, the people are powerfully built, and we saw some of the Anakim there, descendants of the ancient race of giants. We felt like grasshoppers before them, they were so tall.*

Despite the fact that the Israelites had lived through the *great escape* from Egypt with Moses and had witnessed the miraculous power and deliverance from God their mindset had not changed. They still had a slave mentality whereby they could not perceive themselves as victors and able to defeat their enemies. They saw themselves as victims who were intimidated by what they could see. They saw themselves as grasshoppers and were defeatists. They forgot the promise that was given to them many years before and although the promise was being manifested to them and they had clear evidence from the grapes they had bought back. They did not have the capacity to receive the promise as it was not being mixed with faith. They did not grow from their experiences of deliverance from Egypt or from God sustaining them whilst they were in the wilderness. They did not understand that although God had promised them the land, they still had to take action and possess it, which they were refusing to do. They refused to co-operate.

Caleb and the other spy, Joshua, had a completely different mindset. They focused on the God who had made the promise that they would inherit the land and they remembered God's work of deliverance. They continued to reassure the people.

Numbers 14:7–8

> ...It is a wonderful country ahead, and the Lord loves us. He will bring us safely into the land and give it to us. It is a very fertile land flowing with milk and honey.

God's word and promises must be mixed with faith in order for the promises to come to fruition. There are many times when God's promises are not fulfilled in our lives because we have not had faith or believed that He would fulfil them. If the promise is not mixed with faith, then how can it come to fruition, just like a seed that is not planted and nurtured, it will never grow.

God needs us to co-operate and work with Him and that takes place when we come into alignment with Him and His word. Therefore, when we come to Christ, our mindset needs to change. This occurs through faith, the work of the Holy Spirit and application of the word of God.

Hebrews 4:2

*For this wonderful news – the message that God wants to save us – has been given to us just as it was given to those who lived in the time of Moses. But it didn't do them any good because they did not believe it. They didn't mix it with faith.*

The process of being aligned and assigned is imperative because it determines what we accomplish in life. As we grow and we align ourselves with and apply His word to our lives, change will come. Every *pothole* we hit in life will help to shape us and prepare us for our assignments. It is notable that in the case of Joshua, he became Moses' successor.

The people who aligned themselves with the negative report ended up demanding that they return back to slavery in Egypt.

Numbers 14:3

*The idea swept the camp. "Let's elect a leader to take us back to Egypt" they shouted.*

All the spies that went out were exposed to the same conditions. They all saw the same things, but they had different perspectives that resulted in different outcomes. The final outcome was very sad in that God said Joshua and Caleb would inherit the land but, because of the negative responses and negative accusations made against Him, no one else from that generation would. Subsequently they roamed around in the wilderness for forty long years until they had all passed away. The promise of inheriting the land was given again to the next generation.

Deuteronomy 7:22–23

> *He will cast them out a little at a time; he will not do it all at once, for if he did, the wild animals would multiply too quickly and become dangerous.*
>
> *He will do it gradually, and you will move in against those nations and destroy them.*

God was true to His word and the next generation did inherit the land. They arrived at a place where they corporately mixed the word of God with their faith and achieved many successes, one of which was Jericho City. Subsequently, they now had the capacity to absorb the promises God had in store for them.

Hebrews 11:30

> *It was faith that brought the walls of Jericho tumbling down after the people of Israel had walked around them seven days, as God had commanded them.*

Unfortunately, due to disobedience and being out of alignment with God's commandments over many years, the children of Israel lost the land again. They did not learn from their experiences or the experiences of their predecessors.

I am pleased to say this was not the case with us. Through learning, growing and trusting in the Lord, we adopted a totally different attitude when we decided to move again. My husband was happy for me to commence the search for a new property as I had more free time than he did. I was also now at a place where I was ready and prepared to believe God and take Him at His word. I had come into a place of alignment and had the capacity to receive whatever God had in store for us. Firstly, I prayed about the matter. I then began to prepare our existing house in order to put it on the market. This involved redecorating and upgrading parts of the house. I then began to look at what properties were available on the market. There were few at the time, but I did not become frustrated, I just waited patiently. One day I decided to go to my local town centre, I browsed at properties in various estate agent's windows and then I saw a property. The advert stated that the house was *Coming to the market soon* so there were no full property details available. I made an inquiry and was told that the property had a viewing over the weekend and was now sold. I asked if I could still arrange a viewing and the agents agreed.

When I arrived at the property there was clearly some work that needed to be done on the exterior of the property. When I stepped through the front door, I knew it was for us. I love old properties with character and this property had fireplaces, a large kitchen diner, nice garden and panoramic views. As I walked into each room, I could visualise our family in the house.

I then arranged for my husband to view the property a few days later and he too really liked the house. Even though we were told the house was sold, I remember thinking if that house is for us, we will have it and there was an element of peace about the whole situation.

A few days later, I received a phone call from the agent. After some pleasantries, he informed me that the person who had made an offer on the house at the weekend had decided that she did not want it, so if I wanted it, it was mine as there had been no other viewings. I was not surprised as I knew that God was on the job. The power of alignment with God and His word brings peace, joy and contentment.

We all experience challenges in life that are really difficult at times. There will be times when you feel like you are in the midst of a storm. However, to have the assurance that God is there every step of the way makes that storm much more bearable. Even a storm does not last forever.

As we grow and develop our relationship with Jesus Christ through reading His word, studying His word and surrendering our will to Him, He begins to reveal more of Himself to us. Just like any other relationship we encounter in life, the more time you spend with a person the more you get to know them. However, in addition to spending more time with Christ, we also get to know more about ourselves and the purposes and plans He has for our lives.

There were some special characters in the Bible that had a deep relationship with God that enabled them to do some extraordinary things as they came into alignment with Him. They were then able to complete their assignments and accomplish God's purposes and plans for their lives. Abraham is called a *Friend of God* in James 3:23 (KJV), David is said to be a man after God's heart (Acts:22) and Mary, the mother of Jesus, is said to be *blessed among women* and had found favour with God (Luke 1:28 &30).

God is still seeking for individuals who want to come into alignment with Him and His word. He still wants to impact lives and He still wants people who are willing to complete assignments for Him so that great things can be accomplished today and forevermore. The wonderful thing is that we are all unique and we should not think, *I can never be like Moses, Abraham or David* – however, we can learn a lot from them. God does not want us to be like them, He wants us to be us and He can use us, just like He used them and many others.

Hebrews 13:8 (KJV)

*Jesus Christ is the same yesterday, and today, and forever.*

The common denominator in their relationship with God is that they were willing to listen and respond to the call of God upon their lives. There was a reciprocal relationship as they came into alignment with Him. It was not a matter of God giving and them taking all the time. Regardless of who you are, we all know such relationships are not sustainable as the giver will eventually ask the question, *Why is it always me that's giving and you are always taking?* My husband has another wise saying, *People want the benefits without the commitment,* and this can be applied to every scenario that involves a relationship. If it is one-sided, it will not last.

## No Condemnation

There's no condemnation to those who believe
Jesus the Saviour paid for our sins.
The tempter comes to steal all that was freely given.

Look up to the cross Look to amazing grace Look to mercy
Look straight at our Saviour's face

Encounter His love that lead him humbly along
He saw our need, which only spurred him on
To Calvary He took all of our wrong doings,
disgrace, shame and murder and the list goes on.

He bore it glady, though the price was so high
But it could not dissuade Him from giving up His own life,
To first please His Father to save you and I.

What passion and love filled His heavy heart?
Yet they parted his garments, scoffing as they cast lots.

He suffered so deeply, so we could be free
There is no condemnation not for you neither me
All He requires is for you to believe

**H. Henry**

# Chapter Eight

## What about our Assignment and Children?

As previously stated, we have been blessed with two lovely sons. Our first child was born four years after we were married. My husband wanted to wait to have children as he took the responsibility of becoming a father very seriously.

Our first child was extremely energetic and challenging and we were not prepared for what was to come. He did not sleep very much, and we spent many nights driving around our neighbourhood trying to get him to sleep. Ironically, he still enjoys driving around at the age of twenty-two, except he can now drive himself.

His personality shone through at a very early age. I remember when his child-minder informed us that of the three children she cared for, our son was the only one who would not take an afternoon nap and he was under the age of one. I used to feel guilty about that, as he made her work for her money as he had to be supervised for the whole day. He also began walking at nine months. When he was two years old, I decided to work part-time and I was shocked at the amount of energy he had, he just never seemed to be tired no matter what activity he was engaged in.

He was the complete opposite of myself and my husband. We were quiet and relaxed, and he was boisterous and loud. When I observed other well-behaved and polite children, I felt guilty and embarrassed as I had difficulty controlling him at times. This was exacerbated when other people commented on my son's hyperactive behaviour. This made me feel even more incompetent. I felt like a failure and many times my husband would have to reassure me and state that our son's behaviour was not a reflection of our parenting and that, *he has his own personality.* This helped to release me from my feelings of incompetence and guilt.

During a conversation with his god-mother one day, I explained his hyperactive behaviour to her and she said something that resonated with me immediately. She said, *"Do not try to change him and make him have a personality like you and his father, God has given him that personality for a reason. You don't know what he will become in the future so don't change him."* I was stunned and did not know what to say but I knew what she had said was right and I needed to hear those words. It is amazing because those words completely changed my perspective on my parenting and helped me to see my son as God saw him and that He had created him that way for a reason.

Sometimes we just need to hear words of wisdom and encouragement. After I received those words, I felt a complete release. Instead of trying to get my son to conform to who I thought he should be, I looked at him in a different way. I began to observe his talents and skills and therefore, sought to nurture and provide opportunities for him to express himself rather than limit him. I realised that he needed a structured environment and we also discovered that he liked to play and watch football. Consequently, we actively sought out football clubs for him to attend from the age of four onwards.

This helped to re-direct his energy in a positive way and as he grew older, he played football for his school, local clubs and then went onto to play for an academy up to until the age of sixteen.

I now know why he had so much energy and why he has the personality that he has. He obtained eleven GCSE's whilst attending school only four days per week for the last two years of school, as he spent one day a week at the football academy. He left home at the age of sixteen and went to live with another family whilst he was studying and playing football. He then signed a football contract. He then left that club and went to the USA on a full football scholarship to live and study and all of this was before the age of twenty-one.

He had to have a resilient personality and have the confidence and energy to achieve all of this. When I share this story with people, they are often amazed and it is only when I see or hear their response that I think that it is only by the grace of God that he has experienced a lot more than someone else of his age.

Experiences can help navigate someone else on their journey in life and help them to come into alignment and accomplish great things and you, too, can be a part of their story. I know that if I had not been aligned with God's word and completed various assignments myself or accomplished certain things, I probably would have struggled to let my son leave home at that age. Despite my own needs or insecurities, and because I know the God in whom I trust has plans to give us a hope and a future, I could let him go.

We have another son who is five years younger and we observed that he too liked football. One might say this was a natural progression because of his older brother. However, this was not the case as five years difference between two siblings is quite significant. His personality is also very different to his brother. He was a quiet, compliant child and did not present much challenging behaviour. Once again, we sought to get him involved in a football club from the age of four years old and he too played for his local team and school teams. He too attended an academy and likewise, passed all eleven of his GCSE's and has since had the opportunity to leave home and attend a football academy abroad at the age of sixteen.

If you have children or are in contact with children, observe them. Observe their gifts, talents and personalities from an early age. If you identify something that they enjoy doing or that comes natural to them encourage them, nurture them, provide the opportunities for them to develop their skills or passions. Who knows where that gift or talent might take them, who knows what doors might open up to them.

This is why it is important to come into alignment and complete your assignments because it is not just about you, it is about others around you who you could potentially influence and inspire. It may be your own child, a child at school, a relative, a god-child, or a child who attends Sunday school.

It is imperative to state that it is very difficult to help others if you have refused to align yourself with God and His word. This would affect your ability to complete the assignments God has for you and inadvertently affect what you accomplish in this life. I am not saying that you would be unsuccessful, but you would not be fulfilling your true God-intended potential.

There is a woman in the Bible called Hannah. 1 Samuel 1:1–26 outlines her story. She was desperate to have a child but was unable to. She cried out to God in agony and desperation.

1 Samuel 1: 9–11

> *One evening after supper, when they were in Shiloh, Hannah went over to the Tabernacle. Eli the priest was sitting at his customary place beside the entrance.*
>
> *She was in deep anguish and was crying bitterly as she prayed to the Lord. And she made this vow: "O Lord of heaven, if you will look down upon my sorrow and answer my prayer and give me a son, then I will give him back to you, and he'll be yours for his entire lifetime, and his hair shall never be cut."*

Hannah was clearly broken and cried out to the one whom she believed could help her. She was so desperate to have a child, that she promised God if He gave her a child, she would give him back to God. That could not have been an easy prayer for Hannah, but she was willing to let go and let God have His way in her life. Hannah was willing to let God be in the driving seat of her life. Even in her anguish, God was at work. As Hannah was praying at the Tabernacle, Eli, the priest, saw her. He thought she was a drunken woman.

1 Samuel 1: 12-14

*Eli noticed her mouth moving as she was praying silently and, hearing no sound, thought she had been drinking.*

*"Must you come here drunk?" he demanded. "Throw away your bottle."*

Eli the priest was out of alignment with God. His family had been part of the priesthood for generations. He and his sons were now so far removed from God they were not fulfilling their assignments and were unable to accomplish God's will. Eli was unable to discern Hannah's cry of desperation and assumed she was drunk. The priesthood had fallen into a state of degradation. The very priests who should have been examples and God's representatives abused their position of power and stole the offerings that were meant to be for God and were seducing the young women.

1 Samuel 2:12&17

*Now the sons of Eli were evil men who didn't love the Lord.*

*So, the sin of these young men was very great in the eyes of the Lord; for they treated the people's offering to the Lord with contempt.*

When you love God your attitude and behaviour reflects this. These men clearly did not love God and the fruits of their labour showed this. These men were in prominent positions. They were fulfilling their obligations in their own way, which was clearly out of alignment with God's way. In their eyes they probably thought that they could not be challenged because of their heritage and responsibilities. They refused to listen to their father, Eli, when he tried to admonish them. However, God is not a *put up and shut up* kind of God, especially if you are meant to be a representative of His. He had a plan to deal with this and he had an assignment for Hannah. Hannah became pregnant the following year, and she fulfilled her promise.

1 Samuel 1:26–28

*"Sir, do you remember me?" Hannah asked him. "I am the woman who stood here that time praying to the Lord.*

*I asked him to give me this child, and he has given me my request;*

*and now I am giving him to the Lord for as long as he lives." So, she left him there at the Tabernacle for the Lord to use.*

Hannah visited Samuel every year and gave him a little linen robe just like the priests wore. She maintained contact with him, so he would have had a relationship with her and knew she was his mother. Hannah was so grateful that God heard and answered her prayer, she was therefore, more than willing to fulfill her promise.

I can only imagine the conversations they probably had as a mother and child. I am sure Samuel would have asked loads of questions as he grew older including, *Why do I live here? or why can't I go back with you?* As Hannah was in alignment with God's word, she probably told Samuel how special he was; how she had prayed for a child and God answered her prayer by blessing her with him. She probably told him about the promise that she had made to God and how she had honoured that promise. Maybe she shared how God had chosen him (Samuel) to help Eli the priest and what a special blessing and privilege that was. Hannah reinforced his role of being involved in the priesthood by providing Samuel with a little robe every year just like the other priests wore as he was being prepared and disciplined for the ministry.

Proverbs 22:6 (KJV)

*Train up a child in the way he should go: and when he is old, he will not depart from it.*

The above Scripture was written many years later by king Solomon. Hannah however, already had this revelation decades earlier. She had made a promise that she was going to give her child back to God and the best place for that was to place him in the temple of God with the priests. This would allow him to be exposed to the presence of God and also learn about the priesthood.

Eli and his sons were not positive role models. Therefore, God devised a plan where He, Himself, would be Samuel's mentor and therefore, spoke to him directly. God had warned Eli about the dishonour he and his sons had shown him. He would now remove them from office and a message was sent to Eli to confirm this.

1 Samuel 2:35 (KJV)

> *And I will raise me up a faithful priest, that shall do according to that which is in mine heart and in my mind: and I will build him a sure house; and he shall walk before mine anointed for ever.*

God needed a vessel to enable this *faithful priest* to be born. There is no coincidence why Hannah was chosen. When you read about Hannah you can almost feel the sincerity and burden of Hannah's heart. God placed that burden inside of her and she was the perfect person to carry out the assignment. Hannah made a promise and fulfilled HER promise to God not knowing if she was ever going to have another child. God honoured her words and actions and she was later blessed with three other sons and two daughters. The mission was accomplished. God had his *faithful priest* and Hannah had more children.

Samuel was called by God as a young man. He was called audibly one night by God after the lamp went out in the temple as Eli was by now almost blind. Samuel thought he heard Eli call him on three occasions in one night. On each occasion Samuel went to Eli and said, *Here I am.* (1 Samuel 3:2-10) Samuel demonstrated that he had a servant's heart.

Some children would have become frustrated after the first call and probably would have thought, *Why should I get out of my bed again,* and most likely would have ignored the voice after the second time, but not Samuel. God knew his heart.

Eventually Eli realised it was God who was calling Samuel and he advised him that if he heard the voice again, he should say:

1 Samuel 3:9 (KJV)

> *...Speak Lord; for thy servant heareth.*

The Lord did call Samuel again and he responded once again with a servant's heart. Once Samuel responded to God's call upon his life, God used Samuel mightily in Israel for decades. He was a prophet, priest, leader and a judge over Israel and was used to anoint and appoint kings in Israel. God's plan for replacing the existing priesthood was assigned to Samuel and he remained faithful, successfully accomplishing what God wanted him to achieve.

We can learn a lesson from Hannah's actions regarding Samuel. She placed him in an environment where she was able to fulfill her promise and where God was able to teach him and use Samuel to fulfill His purpose.

It is important that whatever God has placed within us regarding our gifts, talents and purpose, we are in an environment where these can be fulfilled and exercised. We can also seek to educate ourselves and reaffirm what God wants from us. For example, if you believe God has given you a heart for children, then look for opportunities where you can work with children. If you believe God has given you a heart for the homeless, then find organisations that work with the homeless or better still volunteer your services to help. The same principle applies to setting up a business or even writing a book.

If Samuel had not been in the temple assisting Eli, he may not have understood that God was calling him. It was Eli who discerned it was God calling Samuel and Eli advised him to answer, *Yes Lord, thy servant heareth.* Similarly, if Moses had continued to live in the mountain and had not gone to Egypt, he could not have fulfilled God's purpose of being a freedom fighter for the Israelite slaves. If Nehemiah had remained in the presence of the king and had not gone back to Jerusalem, he could not have orchestrated the rebuilding of the wall. If Abigail had remained in her environment and had not gone out to meet David, she would not have saved her family and prevented David from committing an act he probably would have regretted.

They all had to be in the right environment or within the proximity of their calling to make an impact and bring about change. As the saying goes, t*o do the same thing and expect different results is madness.* It could also be said that to remain in the same environment or even the same mindset and expect different results, is madness too. We need to step out into a new environment and change our mindset in order to fulfill whatever it is God wants us to fulfill. After all, the glory will inevitably go back to God because we know that without Him, we can do nothing.

# Identity

*Do you know who you are and were created to be?*
*Do you know what it cost to set you free?*
*I went to the cross to save your soul*
*But not only that, to make you whole.*


*I was stripped, whipped and lashed*
*But I knew I must endure,*
*I saw you whilst you were yet sinners,*
*Only my shed blood could unlock the door.*

*Do you see my pain when you deny? Who I've made you,*
*So why do you cry?*
*Why do you savour and listen to the voice of evil persuasion?*

*Your identity is hidden in me*
*Kings and priests are who I see*
*Clothed in raiment white and pure.*
*Come take your sonship, I am the door....*
*Seek for me, I knock gently on your heart...*
*I can promise you; I will never depart.*
*Put trust in me, I have your identity,*
*written into your eternity.*

**H. Henry**

# Chapter Nine

## The Outcome of the Assignment

The power of the environment can influence the outcome of the assignment.

In the previous chapter, we looked at the impact of being in the right environment in order to complete the assignment. I want to explore this in more detail by closely examining a few characters from the book of Esther.

Esther was a young Jewish woman who lived during the era when the Persian Empire was at its height. It ruled over one hundred and twenty-seven provinces; from India to Ethiopia. The Jewish people who lived in these provinces at the time, sought to maintain their faith and traditions. It appears this was accepted as long as it did not pose a threat to the ruling monarchy.

Esther was a Jewish orphan and was raised by her cousin Mordecai, who raised her as his own daughter. The Bible described her to be a very beautiful woman.

King Ahasuerus of the Persians had a state celebration and he invited a number of officials from all over his empire. The celebration lasted six months and was a great display of the wealth and success of the empire. After the six months celebration had ended, the king arranged a further celebration for the people who were in the palace of Shushan (within the borders of Iran). The king had a very beautiful wife called, Vashti. She too arranged a party for the women of the palace at the same time as the king.

On the seventh day of the celebration the king sent his royal officials to ask queen Vashti to join him so that he could show off her beauty.

She refused his request. It is not known why she refused but the headline was that she clearly and publicly disobeyed the king. This was not acceptable; consequently, she was made an example of and was banished from the kingdom.

On the surface, this judgment appears harsh. It is important to understand the concept and context of what it meant to live in a kingdom and under the rule of a king. The late David Pawson was a renowned teacher, author and speaker and has studied the topic of The Kingdom of God. He provides some very interesting insight on the topic. (www.davidpawson.org web 1 June 2020)

Pawson explains that historically the world was ruled by different kings that had sovereign control and authority over their jurisdictions or empires. Within such kingdoms the king owned everything including the land; sometimes being referred to as lord (shortened version of landlord). Within the kingdom were subjects (people). The king did not rule according to any ideology such as governmental democracy, socialism or even communism. In the kingdom, the king's word was the final word of authority and once his word was given, he could not reverse it. Therefore, no one had the right to challenge the word of the king.

The late Dr Myles Munroe gave this definition of a kingdom:

*A kingdom is the governing influence of a king over his territory, impacting it with his personal will, purpose and intent, producing a culture, values, morals, and lifestyle that reflect the king's desires and nature for his citizens.* (Munroe 2006, Kingdom Principles, Preparing for Kingdom Experience and Expansion p,36)

With this understanding we can see why queen Vashti was removed from her position as queen. Her attitude and response had undermined the king and would have spread throughout the whole kingdom. Subsequently, as the saying goes, the king *dealt with the acorn before it became an oak tree.*

King Ahasuerus wanted a queen to replace Vashti and so a number of women were taken to his palace grounds in Shushan where they received twelve months of beauty treatments. Esther was one of those women and she was eventually chosen to be the replacement queen. Whilst she was in the palace, Esther was shown favour by the palace officials. She was treated extremely well. She was told by Mordecai not to reveal her Jewish heritage at that time.

Then Mordecai happened to be in the right place at the right time. He heard two of the king's guards, planning to assassinate the king. Due to Esther being the queen and his proximity to her, Mordecai was able to get a message to her to warn the king. The culprits were dealt with and the king's life was saved.

Mordecai was clearly a man who held on to his Jewish heritage and traditions and this infuriated Haman, who was one of the king's most powerful officials. The king had commanded that all the other officials should bow to him in order to show reverence to him. Mordecai refused as this was contrary to his Jewish belief, and this outraged Haman. He felt disrespected and as a consequence decided that he would not only deal with Mordecai on this issue, but with the whole of Mordecai's people, namely, the Jews. He devised a wicked plan whereby he would deceitfully obtain the king's consent for the whole of the Jewish people throughout all the provinces to be annihilated.

Esther 3:8

> Haman now approached the king about the matter. "There is a certain race of people scattered through all the provinces of your kingdom," he began, "and their laws are different from those of any other nation, they refuse to obey the king's law; therefore, it is not in the kings interest to let them live..."

Later it all became clear that God had an assignment for Esther. He needed her to be in a position of power and influence. The best way to achieve this, was to place her in the environment of the palace and within close proximity to the king. Given Esther's personality, she was an obedient woman, who listened and took advice, she never thought to herself, *Now I am queen I don't need to listen to Mordecai anymore.* She did not ignore or isolate herself from Mordecai but continued to maintain a relationship with him the best way she could under the circumstances.

The Bible is clear in stating that both queen Vashti and queen Esther were beautiful women, but there was a clear difference in their personalities. Vashti appears to have perceived herself as being on par with the king and so felt she had the right to challenge his word. Esther, on the other hand, recognised that although she was the queen she was aware of the parameters in which she could operate. Power affects different people in different ways.

Someone once told me that if you are thinking of marrying someone, whatever you see in the beginning, expect more of it at the end. Do not think that you will have the power to change them because it is unlikely that you will. Therefore, if you see things you can not live with then do not marry him/her. You could save yourself a lot of problems. In contrast to this if you see qualities you do like then expect more from that person. In the case of queen Esther, prior to her entering the palace, she showed honour, obedience and respect and accepted advice from Mordecai and others. These attributes continued and transcended into all her relationships, as they were a part of her character.

Esther 2:15
> *When it was Esther's turn to go to the king, she accepted the advice of Hegai, the eunuch in charge of the harem, dressing according to his instructions. And all the other girls exclaimed with delight when they saw her.*

We can see that Mordecai is clearly a man of integrity and is not willing to compromise who he is and what he believes. Whilst all the other officials were paying homage to Haman's ego, he was not prepared to entertain it.

Unfortunately, there are many individuals who, once they have been promoted and are successful, forget who they are and where they came from. Some people also become so obsessed with power that they seek to control or destroy anyone who stands in their way. Haman was clearly such an individual. He was motivated by power and control and therefore deceitfully orchestrated the death penalty for all of the Jews. After the decree was made, orders were sent throughout the provinces that all the Jews should be killed. When the news reached Mordecai, he was obviously distraught. He tore his clothes and put on sack cloth and ashes and went about the city, wailing and crying, as did other Jews in the other provinces. News finally reached Esther that Mordecai was in mourning because of the decree.

### Esther 4:8

> *Mordecai also gave Hathach a copy of the king's decree dooming all Jews, and told him to show it to Esther and to tell her what was happening, and that she should go to the king to plead for her people.*

Esther was fully aware of what had happened to her predecessor, Vashti. She had not been invited to enter into the king's presence for over a month and knew the risks involved if she or anyone else invited themselves into his presence. However, Mordecai knew that this was literally a life or death situation.

Esther 4:13–14

*This was Mordecai's reply to Esther: "Do you think you will escape there in the palace, when all other Jews are killed?*

*If you keep quiet at a time like this, God will deliver the Jews from some other source, but you and your relatives will die; what's more who can say but that God has brought you into the palace for just such a time as this?"*


I am sure those words pierced Esther's heart, when Mordecai made the statement, *...who can say that God has brought you into the palace for such a time as this.*

The weight of responsibility must have impacted her so much. Esther was now in a position where she had to make a decision. She could either keep quiet and never reveal her heritage to the king, or she could come into alignment with Mordecai's request. Esther takes on board Mordecai's request and makes the dramatic decision to align herself with it. She is prepared to take on the assignment but due to the difficulty and complexity, she requests *back-up*. She sends a message to Mordecai:


Esther 4:16

*Go and gather together all the Jews of Shushan and fast for me; do not eat or drink for three days, night or day; and I and my maids will do the same; and then, though it is strictly forbidden, I will go in to see the king; and if I perish, I perish.*


Esther is now prepared to die for what she believes in order to help save her people. She requests the support of the other Jews in her vicinity; asking them to fast for her. Although she would be the only one approaching the king, she knew she would not be alone, as all the other Jews were with her, not in body but in spirit; empowering her to take on the task.

Esther has her own carefully planned strategy on how to approach the king. She puts on her royal robes and positions herself where she is not imposing but is still close enough for the king to see her. He then invites her into his presence. He then asks her what does she want and at that stage, offers her half of his kingdom. Esther could have disclosed there and then what she wanted, but she does not. Instead she invites king Ahasuerus and Haman to a banquet. They are invited into her presence and into her private environment that she now controls.

Haman, no doubt, feels honoured and really privileged in that he has a special audience with the king *and* the queen. On his return home he sees Mordecai and is enraged that he does not show him reverence.

He explains this to his wife.


Esther 5:12

> ...*Yes, and Esther, the queen, invited only me and the king himself to the banquet she prepared for us; and tomorrow we are invited again.*
>
> *"But yet,"* he added *"all this is nothing when I see Mordecai the Jew just sitting in front of the king's gate, refusing to bow to me."*


Haman's wicked wife and their friends encouraged Haman to build gallows, so that he could hang Mordecai. Haman was in a toxic and dysfunctional environment. There was no one in his inner circle who challenged him or stopped him to at least think about his potential actions and the consequences. In fact, they encouraged him. Haman now had a strategy in place to fulfill his wicked assignment.

Esther 5:14

> *"Well," suggested Zeresh his wife and all his friends, "get ready a 75-foot- high gallows, and in the morning ask the king to let you hang Mordecai on it; and when this is done you can go on your merry way with the king to the banquet." This pleased Haman immensely and he ordered the gallows to be built.*

That night king Ahasuerus has a dream and is reminded about the fact that his life was saved from two men who tried to assassinate him. He asks his servants whether the person who alerted him has ever been rewarded. He is told that it was Mordecai and that he never received a reward.

Consequently, the next morning the king asked who was in the royal court. It happened to be Haman who was seeking permission from the king to hang Mordecai. Haman is brought into the presence of the king. The king asks him, *"How should a man, who pleases his king be honoured?"* Egoistic Haman believes the king is referring to him.

Esther 6:6–9

> *...Haman thought to himself, "Whom would he want to honour more than me?"*
>
> *So he replied, "Bring out some of the royal robes the king himself has worn, and the king's own horse, and the royal crown, and instruct one of the king's most noble princes to*

robe the man and to lead him through the streets on the king's own horse, shouting before him, this is the way the king honours those who truly please him.'"

"Excellent." the king said to Haman. "Hurry and take these robes and my horse and do what you have just said – to Mordecai the Jew, who works at the Chancellery. Follow every detail you have suggested."

A few days before, Mordecai's life hung in the balance. He was in mourning for his life and that of his people. He was literally at the mercy of Haman's wicked plot. However, there was a divine intervention. The king was reminded in a dream that very night, of the role Mordecai played in saving his life. The following day Haman was seeking permission to have Mordecai hanged. God made it possible that Mordecai was rewarded and esteemed by the very person who despised him. That same person who hated him was ordered to march around the streets shouting:

Esther 6:11

> ...this is the way the king honours those who truly please him.

This was a miraculous turnaround of events for Mordecai.

Psalms 75:6–7

> For promotion and power come from nowhere on earth, but only from God.
>
> He promotes one and deposes another.

It probably took Mordecai time to digest what was actually happening as he was being paraded around the streets and being exalted by his enemy. The Bible also reminds us to beware not to align ourselves with evil, as Haman had.

Micah 2:1–2

*Woe to you who lie awake at night, plotting wickedness; you rise at dawn to carry out your schemes; because you can, you do.*

*You want a certain piece of land, or someone elses house (though it is all he has); you take it by fraud and threats and violence.*

Proverbs 26:27

*The man who sets a trap for others will get caught in it himself. Roll a boulder down on someone, and it will roll back and crush you.*

We see the fulfillment of the above when Esther invites Haman and the king to another banquet. Once, again the king asks her, what she desires from him. She discloses her request.

Esther 7:3–6

*And at last queen Esther replied, "If I have won your favour, O king, and if it pleases Your Majesty, save my life and the lives of my people.*

*For I and my people have been sold to those who will destroy us. We are doomed to destruction and slaughter. If we were only to be sold as slaves, perhaps I could remain quiet, though even then there would be incalculable damage to the king that no amount of money could begin to cover."*

*"What are you talking about?" King Ahasuerus demanded. "Who would dare touch you?"*

*Esther replied, "This wicked Haman is our enemy."*

*Then Haman grew pale with fright before the king and queen.*

The very deeds that were being constructed in darkness were now in the light. Imagine the shock on Haman's face when his plan was exposed. He knew that his own life was now in danger and the outcome was going to be fatal for him as stipulated *'the man who sets a trap for others will get caught in it himself...'* (Proverbs 26:27) was now a reality for him as his plan had backfired.

The king was so shocked by what queen Esther had reported to him that he walked out of the room and into the palace garden. It probably took him time to process what had just happened as he had been tricked into placing the life of his beloved wife, the queen and all of her people to a death sentence. This was all instigated by his trusted adviser.

In the meantime, Haman was pleading with queen Esther for his life. The king saw this on his return and ordered that Haman was to be hanged on the gallows that he had prepared for Mordecai.

Mordecai was then appointed in Haman's place and was given responsibility along with Esther to reverse Haman's wicked plot. Due to the extensive empire, there were some casualties as the message had to be spread to all of the one hundred and twenty-seven provinces. Subsequently the Jews also received word that they could defend themselves if they were attacked.

Haman's plot of ethnic cleansing was unsuccessful. If it had succeeded, no one could imagine what the subsequent days would have been like. As his plan failed, the 14$^{th}$ day of the Hebrew month, Adar, is now a day of feasting and celebration as the lives of the Jewish people were saved. At that time Mordecai made a decree that the event should be remembered in a positive way throughout the provinces. This event is still celebrated today in the Jewish culture and is known as the *Feast of Purim*.

It is clear that Haman aligned himself with narcissistic thoughts and beliefs and this in turn influenced his behaviour and actions. He had a deep need for excessive admiration and self-importance and lacked empathy towards others. In contrast to Haman, Mordecai was clearly a man of God, who lived according to the principles of God's word. He recognised that although he was in a foreign land, he chose not to conform to certain principles that violated his own beliefs. He recognised that he was part of a minority group living in an environment that was dominated by foreign Persian culture. Despite being part of a minority, Mordecai was not prepared to conform to that culture at the expense of his own beliefs and identity.

Issues of marginalisation are still relevant today for some of us who choose to align ourselves with God and His word. If we choose not to conform, this can sometimes upset people around us and as a result we may be rejected or labelled as being a *trouble-maker* or identified as someone who does not *fit in*. We are then faced with a choice. Do we try to fit in and lose our identity or do we continue to stand firm and hold to our values and beliefs?

Thank goodness, we can learn from how Jesus handled this situation. He came into an environment that was dominated by the Roman Empire. Although the Jews were still allowed to practice elements of their culture and religious beliefs, there was still an element of oppression by the Romans. For example, the Jews were coerced to pay high taxes and undertake a census. If they did not co-operate there were penalties imposed upon them. In addition to this, as long as the Jews did not threaten the stability of the Roman Empire, they were accepted into society.

When Jesus Christ came on the scene, he clearly did not fit into the environment created by the religious Jewish leaders of the day; the Scribes and the Pharisees. They expected a king to arrive who was full of grandeur and power like king David or king Solomon and someone who would deliver them from the Roman oppression. Jesus came as a humble servant and did not appear to be much of a freedom fighter. However, even though Jesus did not fulfill the expectations of others, people still recognised there was something special about Him, but this was overshadowed by them labelling Him as *the carpenter's son;* resulting in their rejection of Him.

Matthew 13:53-57

> *When Jesus had finished giving these illustrations, he returned to his hometown, Nazareth of Galilee, and taught there in the synagogue and astonished everyone with his wisdom and miracles.*
>
> *"How is this possible?" the people exclaimed. "He's just a carpenter's son, and we know Mary his mother and his brothers- James, Joseph, Simon, and Judas.*
>
> *And his sisters-they all live here. How can he be so great?" And they became angry with Him.*

John 1:11 (KJV)

> *He came unto his own, and his own received him not.*

Despite the Jews rejection of Jesus, He was not intimidated or afraid that He did not fit in with their ideals. On the contrary, He knew who He was, where He came from and where He was going. That helped Him to keep focused on His assignment, which was to draw others into His kingdom, which is not of this world.

John 18:36

> Then Jesus answered, "I am not an earthly king. If I were, my followers would have fought when I was arrested by the Jewish leaders. But my Kingdom is not of the world."
>
> Pilate replied, "But you are a king then?"
>
> "Yes." Jesus said. "I was born for that purpose. And I came to bring truth to the world. All who love the truth are my followers."

Jesus created an environment in which those who sought truth were drawn to Him. Jesus was able to attract people from all walks of life as He ministered, healed, valued, taught and accepted them. Where many of the Jewish leaders had cast judgment and made the people feel worthless, Jesus did the opposite and word quickly spread about His ministry. Jesus now came to show them and teach them about the kingdom where He had come from and that is the kingdom of God.

Luke 9:11

> But the crowds found out where he was going and followed. And he welcomed them, teaching them again about the Kingdom of God and curing those who were ill.

If we choose to live in alignment with God's word and we receive of His spirit, then it is possible that we too can create an environment where His presence is always with us. Jesus explained this to a group of curious Pharisees.

Luke 17:20

> One day the Pharisees asked Jesus, "When will the Kingdom of God begin?" Jesus replied, "The Kingdom of God isn't ushered in with visible signs. You won't be able to say, 'It has begun here in this place or there in that part of the country.' For the Kingdom of God is within you."

Therefore, the kingdom of God is revealed to you when you believe, accept and understand that Jesus Christ is the King of kings and the Lord of lords. Also, when you receive of His Spirit, this enables you to live in accordance with His word and exposes you to the culture of His kingdom as His Spirit now lives within you. Consequently, when you choose to align yourself with the laws of His kingdom, you then become a subject of His kingdom.

Romans 14:17 (KJV)

> For the kingdom of God is not meat and drink; but righteousness, and peace and joy in the Holy Ghost.

This now opens the door for you to experience challenges and difficulties from others who do not understand or who have rejected Christ. As your life is being changed and you now choose to live righteously according to God's laws, they may perceive you to be weak or soft and may even marginalise or criticise you. Jesus warns that this would happen.

John 15:18–19 (NIV)

> ...If the world hates you, keep in mind that it hated me first. If you belonged to the world, it would love you as its own. As it is, you do not belong to the world, but I have chosen you out of the world. That is why the world hates you.

If Mordecai accepted the status quo and showed reverence to Haman he would not have experienced what he experienced. He would not have stood out as he would have conformed to that system. However, as he refused to conform, he was hated by Haman. This is as relevant today as it was all those years ago in the days of Mordecai.

Jesus was also hated because He did not conform to the systems of this world. The reality is that it is impossible to serve in two kingdoms simultaneously. You cannot serve in the kingdom of God and the system of the world at the same time. We all have the opportunity to choose who or what we serve.

Matthew 6:24

> You cannot serve two masters: God and money. For you will hate one and love the other, or else the other way around....

Although this verse is talking about money, it applies to anything or anyone we put before God in our lives. As previously discussed, God wants to be in the driving seat of our lives, and He wants us to trust Him. If someone else is in the driving seat and taking control of the wheel (including ourselves) then that is a choice that we have made. I have never seen two people in the driving seat of one vehicle trying to control it at the same time and I doubt I ever will. Although what I have seen in films (and I stress, *films*) is where a person in the passenger seat stretches across and tries to take control of the steering wheel. However, the outcome has never been good. It usually results in some form of collision.

This chapter demonstrates how three different people, Mordecai, Esther and Haman had three different assignments. Each is influenced by the power of their environment and the outcome of each one is very different. Therefore, we really need to assess the impact of our environment and how this influences us.

Is our environment positive and nurturing where we are surrounded by people who are choosing to live in alignment with God's word? Or are we in a toxic environment full of negativity and criticism where people choose to live out of alignment with the word of God and seek to fulfill their own desires? Are you happy living in the status quo? Only you can answer these questions.

The wonderful thing is that whether we are in a nurturing or toxic environment, as a child of God and being filled with His Spirit, we can take the kingdom of God with us wherever we go as it dwells within us. This means we can create and influence our own environment no matter what is happening around us externally.

I am reminded of an incident in the Bible when Paul and Silas were imprisoned for preaching the gospel. The story continues that after Paul performed a miracle of deliverance for a woman, the established *businessmen* of the town did not appreciate it. Therefore, they went to the magistrates of the town and complained. This resulted in Paul and Silas being beaten and falsely imprisoned (Acts 16:16–24). Under such circumstances one would have thought they would have been proclaiming their innocence and the injustice of the system, but they do not. They knew that they had the power within them to change their environment through the Holy Spirit.

So, with this in mind, we are told in

Acts 16:25-26 (KJV)

*And at midnight Paul and Silas prayed, and sang praises unto God: and the prisoners heard them.*

*And suddenly there was a great earthquake, so that the foundations of the prison were shaken: and immediately all the doors were opened, and everyone's bands were loosed.*

I can only imagine when the other prisoners heard them singing, they probably thought, what on earth are they doing. It was hardly an environment where one would be singing and praying to God. Paul and Silas knew otherwise: they had something that the others did not have. They had the kingdom of God within them and that was something to celebrate.

When they began to offer up praises to God, something miraculous happened. The King and the Creator of the universe commanded the earth to shake and the earth obeyed, so much so that all the prison doors were opened, the chains fell off the prisoners. They were free. The prison guard woke up. When he saw what had happened, he knew that he would be held accountable for allowing the prisoners to escape. He thought his only option was to commit suicide.

Paul called to him before he was able to commit the act and reassured him that none of them had escaped; they were still there. The soldier was so shocked he fell down in front of Paul and Silas and asked what he needed to do to be saved. Right there and then they told him to believe on the Lord Jesus and he and his household would be saved. He did exactly that and he and his family were baptised. What a dramatic turn of events. Who could have imagined that the change of the environment could have resulted in such a powerful outcome.

## It Doesn't Matter

*It doesn't matter what you throw at me*
*It deepens my attraction*
*To Jesus, the King of Kings who has already taken action*

*He'll fight on my behalf*
*Your powers can't distract him*
*As all power was given Him Yours doesn't match His*
*Not even a fraction*

*In fact, what power do you have over those who are hid in Him?*
*You can't touch His redeemed one's*
*We've been anointed by our King.*

*So, get thee behind me, as my Saviour said before*
*He is my example and the root at my very core*
*A follower of Jesus, I am, and always will be*
*So, it's time for you to pack your bags, go runaway and flee.*

**H. Henry**

# Chapter Ten

## Being Out and Coming Back into Alignment.

If we are truly honest with ourselves, we can clearly see to what some people have chosen to align themselves with and the outcome of their life as a result.

Matthew 7:16 (KJV)

*Ye shall know them by their fruits….*

Look at the degenerative state of our society today and look at the fruits that are on display. Almost every news item is bad news; robbery, murder, violence, and abuse etc. I cannot think of any crime that is committed that does not involve a victim who has had to suffer either overtly or covertly.

There are also people that have experienced suffering due to underlying issues that have never been resolved. It could be the sudden loss of a loved one, loss of employment or any other devastating experience. Consequently, they may seek to manage their hurt or pain by aligning themselves with things that bring them immediate gratification, such as taking drugs or drinking alcohol to numb the pain. The sad thing is that this then becomes so destructive that it spirals out of control and they become increasingly dependent on the substance misuse. The drugs and alcohol now control them and they become a slave to it, in other words they become addicted.

There are also individuals who may have had dysfunctional relationships or poor role models and subsequently gravitate to inappropriate groups within society. Primarily because they want to be accepted and identify with a substitute *family,* which fulfills their need to belong and gives them a sense of identity.

Others may have additional issues such as poor mental health or suffer with depression. Many are prescribed anti-depressants that can also lead to prescribed medication dependency. Some people may receive counseling in an attempt to change their mindset or they may be encouraged to undertake practical activities that engage them in the present so that they do not become so overwhelmed and focused on issues of the past. For example, gardening, sewing, woodwork, art, fishing, sport or voluntary work are all activities that are usually deemed to be therapeutic. During this process people sometimes discover gifts and talents of which that they were unaware. It is all about helping them to align with something that is more positive and not self-destructive.

Many of us experience problems in life but the difference is how we choose to deal with them. If we choose to exclude God from our lives, we have no alternative but to seek to resolve our problems independently of Him. We *think* we know what is best for us and use that as a premise to navigate through life.

Unfortunately for us, life is not always kind, so when we hit a *pothole* we do not really know how to deal with it. Subsequently we find ourselves carrying these heavy burdens life throws at us. God reminds us that He cares about us and He does not want us to carry all these issues because He knows that we can be consumed by them and that *our issues* have the potential to destroy us.

1 Peter 5:7

> Let him have all your worries and cares, for he is always thinking about you and watching everything that concerns you.

Many people who are not believers in God will often ask, if there is a God, why does He allow bad things to happen? A whole book can be written on this subject and many already have. However, God is not responsible for every bad thing that happens in our life. Sometimes things happen as a result of the choices we have made in exercising our own free-will. We suffer the consequences of our decisions and actions. God will not stop us from exercising our free will because He did not create us to be robots.

Romans 1:28-30

> So it was that when they gave God up and would not even acknowledge him, God gave them up to doing everything their evil minds could think of.
>
> Their lives became full of every kind of wickedness and sin, of greed and hate, envy, murder fighting, lying, bitterness, and gossip.
>
> They were backbiters, haters of God, insolent, proud, braggarts (boastful about achievements or possessions) always thinking of new ways of sinning and continually being disobedient to their parents.

It is amazing that the Bible is so timeless. That verse of Scripture sounds like events we have heard about on the news or social media. It sounds like the society that we live in today. That information was recorded over two thousand years ago and it is still relevant today.

The reality is that when we refuse to acknowledge God individually and as a nation, He leaves us to our own evil devices as He has no jurisdiction in our lives when we refuse to align with His word.

Jeremiah 17:9-10

> *The heart is the most deceitful thing there is, and desperately wicked. No one can really know how bad it is.*
>
> *Only the Lord knows. He searches all hearts and examines deepest motives so he can give to each person his right reward, according to his- deeds how he has lived.*

In addition to this, sometimes bad things happen due to an attack from Satan.

1 Peter 5:8

> *Be careful – watch out for the attacks from Satan, your great enemy. He prowls around like a hungry, roaring lion, looking for some victim to tear apart.*

Despite these attacks, God gives us strength to overcome, but we need to come into alignment with Him to enable Him to help us. God needs to know that we are inviting Him into our situation. It may be a simple case of calling upon Him and believing that He will help and that He is fighting on our behalf. Once we are in alignment then let the battle begin.

Deuteronomy 20:4 (KJV)

> *For the LORD your God is he that goeth with you, to fight for you against your enemies, to save you.*

Isaiah 43:2

> *When you go through deep waters and great trouble, I will be with you. When you go through rivers of difficulty, you will not drown. When you walk through the fire of oppression, you will not be burned up-the flames will not consume you.*

Many years ago, I attended a seminar by the late Selwyn Hughes who was a great Christian author and speaker. He once said in one of his seminars that counseling can only help the body (the physical senses that help us to interpret and function in this world) and the soul (our mind, feelings, emotions and decision making processes) but only God can deal with the spirit of a person.

The spirit is the part of us where we feel emptiness, a void, or a hole in our lives and thus try to fill that emptiness with something or someone other than God. If we go through the process of repentance (to turn away from what causes offence to God and think differently) and completely change our direction towards God, and we are willing to accept Jesus Christ into our lives, then we can receive the gift of the Holy Spirit. The Holy Spirit enables us to have a relationship with God through prayer and reading His word. Our spirit then comes alive within us and we have a sense of purpose, peace, direction and fulfillment as we become connected to God. This enables us to come back into alignment with Him, which then brings clarity in our lives and of our assignment. We can then accomplish what He wants us to do.

John 8:12

> *Later, in one of his talks, Jesus said to the people, "I am the Light of the world. So, if you follow me, you won't be stumbling in darkness, for living light will flood your path."*

Jesus used very simple analogies to which the everyday person could relate. If a room is not familiar to you and it is dark and the light is switched off, you may stumble around trying to find the light switch. In fact, most hotels and bedrooms have some form of light switch or lamp near the bed so it is not too much of a struggle to turn on the lights for that very reason.

Jesus is the Light of the world and wants to be the Light in our lives. We all experience some kind of challenging or dark situations in our lives. It is at such times that we do not really know what direction to take and we stumble around, searching for a solution. Some of us may have good support networks around us and just about survive. Others may not have any support and consequently fall victim to destructiveness. As Jesus is the Light, He wants to flood our path and give us direction. His ultimate desire is to walk with us daily, so regardless of what we are experiencing, He is right beside us.

Psalms 119:105 (KJV)

> *Thy word is a lamp unto my feet, and a light unto my path.*

I have heard people say that they are afraid of the dark, but I have never heard anyone say they are afraid of the light, unless they have some medical condition and even then, it is not through choice.

There is a wonderful example of someone who was trying to meet a spiritual need (an emptiness that only God could fill) with physical needs (relationships).

John 4:7–18

Soon a Samaritan woman came to draw water, and Jesus asked her for a drink.

He was alone at the time as His disciples had gone into the village to buy some food.

The woman was surprised that a Jew would ask a despised Samaritan for anything-usually they wouldn't even speak to them and she remarked about this to Jesus.

He replied, "If you knew what a wonderful gift God has for you, and who I am, you would ask me for some living water."

"But you don't have a rope or a bucket," she said, "and this is a very deep well. Where would you get this living water?

And besides, are you greater than our ancestor Jacob? How can you offer better water than this which he and his sons and cattle enjoyed?"

Jesus replied that people soon became thirsty again after drinking this water.

"But the water I give them," he said, "becomes a perpetual spring within them, watering them forever with eternal life."

"Please, sir", the woman said, "give me some of that water. Then I'll never be thirsty again and won't have to make this long trip out here every day."

"Go and get your husband," Jesus told her. "But I am not married," the woman replied.

"All too true." Jesus said, "For you have had five husbands, and you aren't married to the man you're living with now."

This woman had had five husbands and was now living with another man who was not her husband. We do not know the circumstances as to what happened to her previous husbands but whatever it was, she had a need and was seeking for something from those relationships. However, those needs were not being met and Jesus knew that.

We all know that water stagnates when it stops flowing freely. It is also associated with environmental hazards as it can harbour bacteria which can cause fatal diseases and in some cases death.

The water that Jesus was offering this woman was an internal supply of living water; water that is constantly flowing like rain or synonymous with taking a shower. Similarly, the Holy Spirit has the power to wash and cleanse us from within, thus making us whole and complete. In the case of this woman, Jesus was saying that she would not have to go to someone else to get whatever it was she was looking for. She would be connected to a well that would never run dry and that connection would be through her accepting Jesus and living in accordance to His word.

By coming into alignment and receiving Jesus, He would lead her and guide her and guide her into all truth, thus meeting all her needs and enabling her to live a life of contentment. She would always feel satisfied and at peace inside as the flowing water removes any debris or issues that may attempt to cause a blockage in her relationship with God. In addition to this, the well of water would spring up so that she could also inherit eternal life. After her encounter with Jesus, the Samaritan woman was clearly excited. She had never heard anything like this before and she wanted to share the good news with the whole village.

John 4:28–30

> *Then the woman left her water pot beside the well and went back to the village and told everyone, "Come and meet a*

> man who told me everything I ever did. Can this be the Messiah?"
>
> So, the people came streaming from the village to see him.

## John 4:39

> Many from the Samaritan village believed he was the Messiah because of the woman's report: He told me everything I ever did.

God wants everyone to experience having that living water springing up from within. Therefore, it is important for us as Christians to share what God has done in our lives with others without discrimination.

## John 4:34

> Then Jesus explained: My nourishment comes from doing the will of God who sent me, and from finishing his work.

The background to this statement was that the disciples of Jesus had returned with some food for Him and they were urging Him to eat. However, Jesus' response was that His satisfaction did not come from eating physical food. It came from doing God's will, which would literally cost Him His life, and serving others as he was the servant King. Likewise, our satisfaction should not come from the physical things of this world but from fulfilling God's will and the purpose He has for our life.

## Matthew 20:28

> ....Your attitude must be like my own, for I the Messiah, did not come to be served, but to serve, and to give my life as a ransom for many.

Jesus could have given up on us and left us to our own destructive devices. He did not have to give His life as a ransom for us but he did. That was His choice because of His love towards us.

As previously stated, this world is becoming more degenerate. No one can deny that. Much of this is due to the fact that we do what we want to do not really thinking about the consequences of our actions or the impact of our decisions upon others.

Judges 21:25 (KJV)

> In those days there was no king in Israel: every man did that which was right in his own eyes.

When people do what they think is right in their own eyes, the result is what we see in society today. This, of course, is all relative and dependent upon everyone's own perspective of what is right. Subsequently, there is no base line or common ground.

When God delivered the children of Israel from slavery, He knew that they were coming out of a system of oppression and idolatry that had been a part of their lives for around four hundred years. God knew that they would need a new code of conduct by which to live. Hence in the Bible, in the books of Exodus, Leviticus and Deuteronomy, God gave the Israelites a number of laws and commandments by which to live. Unfortunately, they chose not to adhere to them, and repeatedly rebelled against these laws to their own detriment. It was not only the people but their leaders, including the monarchy, who rebelled.

There is a king in the Bible; the first king of Israel. He was anointed and appointed by God; his name is king Saul. The account of his inauguration is detailed in 1 Samuel 10. He was anointed with oil and was told by the prophet Samuel (Hannah's son) that God had appointed him (Saul) to be the king and that God was with him.

Before very long, this king did what was right in his own eyes and came out of alignment with God and began to neglect what he had been instructed to do. He overstepped his mark by stepping into a sacred role that was not his. He was told to wait for the prophet, Samuel, for seven days. He refused to wait and then took on a priestly role by offering a sacrifice to God, which was clearly not in his remit.

This may have seemed like a trivial act on king Saul's part, but the consequences were devastating. He had now put his whole dynasty in danger as he was told that as a result of this disobedience, none of his family would inherit his throne.

King Saul was an arrogant man and instead of accepting that he had done wrong, he constantly justified his actions or blamed other people for his decisions. He continued to disobey; so much so that he remained in office as the appointed king, but he was no longer the anointed king. Consequently, God withdrew his presence from him as He cannot be aligned with willful disobedience, rebellion or anything that causes offence to Him. It was now downhill for king Saul as he became a very bitter and jealous man.

1 Samuel 15:23

> ...For rebellion is as bad as the sin of witchcraft, and stubbornness is as bad as worshipping idols. And now

> *because you have rejected the word of Jehovah, he has rejected you from being king.*

1 Samuel 16:14–16

> *But the Spirit of the Lord had left Saul, and instead, the Lord had sent a tormenting spirit that filled him with depression and fear.*
>
> *Some of Saul's aides suggested a cure. "We'll find a good harpist to play for you whenever the tormenting spirit is bothering you," they said. "The harp music will quiet you and you'll be well again."*

Saul spent the rest of his life seeking to kill his successor. He became consumed with hatred, bitterness and resentment and basically had become an instrument of wickedness.

Romans 6:13

> *Do not let any part of your bodies become tools of wickedness, to be used for sinning; but give yourselves completely to God-every part of you-for you are back from death and you want to be tools in the hands of God, to be used for his good purposes.*

It is a terrible thing to be rejected by God or for us to reject Him, especially when He has made it possible for us to know Him and live in harmony with Him. This has to be on His terms not ours. As human beings we are fickle and change our views and opinions like the weather. Therefore, there would be no stability or consistency in our relationship with God if it was governed by us and on our terms. We are very much governed by our feelings and emotions and can become very temperamental at times. Consequently, it can be very difficult for us to engage with others if we are governed by our moods or for us to engage in something if we are not in the mood. My husband has a saying, *the problem with opinions is that everyone has one.* And it is true. How do we decide what is right and what is wrong, particularly if we start from a flawed position? That is why Jesus gave us the base line.

John 14:6 (KJV)
> *Jesus saith unto him, "I am the way, the truth, and the life: no man cometh unto the Father, but by me."*

Therefore, the only way we can gain access to God is through His son, Jesus Christ as he alone paid the price by giving His life so we would be released from the bondage of sin. The only way we can be aligned with God and His word is when we accept Jesus Christ into our lives and agree to come into line with His word and not to rebel against it. He enables us to do this by giving us His Holy Spirit which lives in us and empowers us to live in obedience to His word. This is the same criteria for everyone. However, we still have to agree to this by surrendering our will to Him just as Jesus surrendered His will to God.

Luke 22:41–42 (moments before Jesus was crucified).
> *He walked away, perhaps a stone's throw, and knelt down and prayed this prayer: "Father, if you are willing, please take away this cup of horror from me. But I want your will, not mine."*

This demonstrates the conflict that sometimes arises between what we want and what God wants for our lives. Thus, Jesus Christ can relate to every challenge or emotion that we face and gives us hope that we too can overcome them.

Hebrews 4:15–16

> *This High Priest of ours understands our weaknesses, since he had the same temptations we do, though he never once gave way to them and sinned.*
>
> *So, let us come boldly to the very throne of God and stay there to receive his mercy and to find grace to help us in our times of need.*

It is reassuring to know that when we are misaligned with God, He gives us the opportunity to come back into line with Him and His word. We also need to cooperate with Him during this process. He knows and understands the temptations, disappointments and challenges we face on a day-to-day basis.

1 Corinthians 10:13

> *But remember this – the wrong desires that come into your life aren't anything new and different. Many others have faced exactly the same problems before you. And no temptation is irresistible. You can trust God to keep the temptation from becoming so strong that you can't stand up against it, for he has promised this and will do what he says. He will show you how to escape temptation's power so that you can bear up patiently against it.*

Sometimes when we experience temptations or difficulties in our lives, we can feel isolated and alone. It is at such times that we are most vulnerable because our thinking and behaviour can become irrational.

2 Corinthians 10:5 (KJV)

> *Casting down imaginations, and every high thing that exalteth itself against the knowledge of God, and bringing into captivity every thought to the obedience of Christ.*

Our minds are very powerful and capable of imagining things beyond belief, so much so that it can affect our behaviour and distort our thinking. That is why we are reminded to *cast down* or throw away the imaginations that build themself up against the knowledge of God and what He says. We have to stop our imaginations running away with us because if we do not, our imaginations will be in control of us and that becomes a dangerous place to be in.

When I decided to leave my position of employment, although I knew it was the right thing to do, I still had an element of fear. This was understandable as I had been in some form of employment from the age of sixteen and I had worked for a long time. Other people thought I was crazy and made statements like, *"What about your pension?"* I had to remind myself that God was still in control even though I was no longer employed, and I also had to think about my health.

I found comfort in these words:

Psalms 37:25 (KJV)

> *...I have not seen the righteous forsaken, nor his seed begging bread.*

2 Timothy 1:7 (KJV)

> *For God hath not given us the spirit of fear; but of power, and of love, and of a sound mind.*

It is imperative that we know what God says in His word and believe it. In order to believe it, we have to align with it. The alignment can only come about when we know the source of these words through our relationship with him. Once we are aligned with the source of these words, then we have an assurance that everything will be okay, and we will experience peace and contentment.

In addition to this, it is always good to talk and not internalise things. Just sharing with someone you can trust (including God in prayer) can help to relieve the pressure, and help you come back into alignment. Very often once issues have been discussed, you feel so much lighter as you no longer feel alone and isolated. Also, you sometimes gain another perspective or idea on how to deal with the issue, which would not happen if you did not talk.

Ecclesiastes 4:9–12

> *Two can accomplish more than twice as much as one, for the results can be much better.*
>
> *If one falls, the other pulls him up; but if a man falls when he is alone, he's in trouble.*
>
> *Also, on a cold night, two under a blanket gain warmth from each other, but how can one be warm alone?*
>
> *And one standing alone can be attacked and defeated, but two can stand back-to-back and conquer; three is even better, for a triple-braided cord is not easily broken.*

This is a powerful Scripture and was also written by king Solomon. No one can deny that two is better than one. We all know that when we have been faced with an insurmountable task, to have a helping hand makes it all the more manageable. I have found this particularly with decorating, renovating or even housework. It is also true that twice as much is accomplished.

I have also been part of a *three stranded cord* prayer group outside of my church for the last few years and it has been a mighty blessing. Two friends and I have gathered together at least once a week to pray, walk, talk and encourage each other and we have seen God answer our prayers. In fact, there was an occasion where one member of our group became ill and was admitted to hospital and her first comment was, *"Nothing changes, we still pray."* We continued to visit her in the hospital and prayed at her bedside. Our friend was a witness and testimony for others as she continued to minister and encourage other patients and nurses on the ward. God has done an amazing work in her life and she has since fully recovered and continues to praise God and live as a witness of His healing power.

The beauty of a three stranded cord prayer group is that if someone is unavailable or away on holiday the other two will continue to pray. I would encourage everyone to be involved in a prayer group like this not as a replacement to local church meetings but in addition to it, as it enhances your spiritual life, and after all you can never pray too much. It is wonderful to pray with likeminded people and it also establishes accountability and helps to keep us in alignment with God's word.

## No More Looking Back.

*No more looking back,*
*I press on the upward track.*
*Looking onto Jesus who holds the true facts.*

*No longer the same,*
*Not playing the devil's game!*
*Moving on from whence I began,*
*From the turning away and being plagued by the shame.*

*Unforgivable…I thought!*
*My guilt grew deeper…cold unresponsive, I started to whimper*
*My accuser alive and full of hate*
*Would have chewed me up and said "Ha, Ha that was fate"*

*But there you are, were and will be*
*Help me continue to look unto thee.*
*My lover, my friend and my everything!*
*My strength and Saviour and wind beneath my wings.*
*No more looking back, I look forward to spring.*
*New life, new hope, new everything!*

**H. Henry**

# Chapter Eleven

## Putting the 3 A's Together.

I conclude with a testimony that demonstrates what happens when one comes into alignment with the word of God and then accepts the allocated assignment. It is amazing to see what God is able to accomplish in and through us.

A friend I had not seen or spoken to for a few years phoned me out of the blue around the time when I started to write this book. I had a couple of missed calls from her and then I made an attempt to call her and fortunately, she answered. After some small talk and general catching up she said that she had been in prayer and the Lord had spoken to her about me. He gave her a message that it was time for me to fulfill my purpose and that there was a call on my life to help people off the streets and bring them into the house of the Lord and that He would show me who to speak to.

I have to say that I was not shocked by this message as it confirmed what had been happening already. I had noticed over the last few years that I was talking to more people and sharing my faith in everyday situations. I had also been involved in feeding the homeless with a friend that year and this had given us the opportunity to talk about Jesus and pray with them. My friend and I had also been concerned about the level of violent crime in our city and were praying about how we could help young people achieve their potential and fulfill their purpose.

I thanked my friend for her phone call and thanked God for confirming what was happening. It confirmed that I was on the right track and in alignment with what God wanted me to do. The following week happened to be the last Friday of the month, which also happened to be our church ladies night where we meet and discuss topics relevant to our faith.

Earlier that day I had been to the gym and when I returned home, the Holy Spirt said to me "Put the seats in the car." I have a 7-seater vehicle that can be used as a van once the seats are taken out. My husband had taken out four of the seats to transport some large items a few weeks before and had not had the time to put them back. My response to that voice was that they are too heavy, and I'll wait for my husband to come home so he can put them in. However, I had another urging to put them in immediately. I thought, okay I will, so I got the wheelbarrow and wheeled each individual seat to the car. To my amazement what was usually an arduous task that resulted in fiddling around and fighting to get the seats into position and subsequently breaking out in a sweat, proved straightforward and easy. They just seemed to slot into position. I even had the time to clean out the car and take it to the car wash before going out with my friend to feed the homeless.

When I returned home, I had a few hours to spare before going to the ladies meeting. Prior to the meeting I received a text from one of the regular attendees stating that she was unable to attend as she was not well. She would usually take other members home after the meeting as they lived near her.

When I arrived at the meeting, I noticed that there were two other ladies there, one had not attended for some time due to other commitments beyond her control, and the other had not visited over the last couple of years. The topic for discussion that evening was, *Finding God's Will*. The opening statement in the booklet was, *God is more interested in our knowing and doing His will than we are in discovering it. He is not trying to hide His will from us. His will is never in opposition to His Word.*

One of the readings was taken from

Philippians 4:6–7 (KJV)

*Be careful for nothing; but in everything by prayer and supplication and with thanksgiving let your requests be made known unto God.*

*And the peace of God which passeth all understanding shall keep your hearts and minds through Christ Jesus.*

The Living Bible puts it like this:

*Don't worry about anything; instead, pray about everything; tell God your needs and don't forget to thank him for his answers.*

*If you do this you will experience God's peace, which is far more wonderful than the human mind can understand. His peace will keep your thoughts and your hearts quiet and at rest as you trust in Christ Jesus.*

Well as you can imagine, it was a very interesting topic for discussion and was in line with a series of preaching and teaching sessions we had had over the last year or so at church. We had teachings on fulfilling your purpose, finding out the gifts and talents that have been given to you, and then more recently, topics on the expression in the vessel. How God wants to express Himself through us as individuals to other individuals who do not know Him. Overall, we were encouraged to find out about our gifts and talents.

Matthew 7:7-8 (KJV)

*Ask and it shall be given you; seek, and ye shall find: knock, and it shall be opened unto you:*

*For every one that asketh receiveth; and he that seeketh findeth; and to him that knocketh it shall be opened.*

These verses highlight that we need to be proactive. If we want something, we need to take action and this is true for everything in life. So, if we want to know our purpose or what our gifts and talents are, we just need to ask. God will answer. He will show us or open up opportunities for us to discover what our gifts and talents are and what He wants us to do with them. As previously stated, we all have free-will and we are free to choose whether we ask or not. Many people who have discovered their gifts and talents often comment that although it may involve work of some sort, it does not feel like work as they enjoy the task so much. They also comment that it is something that they enjoy getting up for in the morning and it gives them motivation and excites them. Some people even say, *"This is what I was born to do."* This takes us right back to living an abundant life.

The ladies meeting finished at around nine o'clock which was earlier than expected. I informed everyone at that point that I would be rushing off as I had some friends visiting the following day and therefore, would not be staying for refreshments. I informed four of the women that I would take them home in the absence of the member who was unable to attend the meeting. As I was getting my belongings together, I was stopped by three people. Two just wanted to talk to me and the third requested prayer. We prayed and then I took the ladies home. By this time, it was approaching ten o'clock.

As I returned home, it was approaching eleven o'clock and beginning to rain. I was about three miles from home when I saw a young woman walking with a push chair, a suitcase and also a phone in her hand. The Holy Spirit said, "Ask her if she is okay."

There was another voice that said, "She's alright, she's probably walking to the train station or phoning for an Uber - Just go home."

As I drove past I felt an urgency inside and the voice again said, "Ask her if she is okay." I continued to drive as I was on a dual carriageway and said in my mind, Okay, I will drive on and then turn round and if she is still there I will ask her.

I continued to drive for about two hundred yards. I turned around and saw that she was still there. I wound my window down on the passenger side and asked, "Hi, are you okay?" Her immediate response was, "No" and she began to cry. She explained that she was staying with a friend with her three-month old and the friend was fed up of hearing her baby cry, so she had told her to leave the house.

It was now just after eleven o'clock and obviously dark and now raining quite heavily. The young woman was trying to phone Women's Aid but could not get through and her phone was about to run out of battery. She said she had nowhere to go and did not know what to do. Although I was shocked, I felt a sense of peace. I told her not to worry and to get in the car with her baby and all her belongings. I then asked her for the number for Women's Aid, which I dialed but did not get through.

I could not remember the number for the non-emergency Police so I said, "This is an emergency, so we need to call the Police" to which she agreed. Just prior to making the call she explained the reason why she was staying with her friend. She was fleeing domestic violence and the matter was also in the hands of the Police and was due to go to Court imminently. She was engaged to the perpetrator but said that his behaviour changed towards her after she had their baby. She also did not have any family members who lived close by.

After we called the Police they asked if she could get to the Central Police station, which was about a mile away. I offered to take her there. She was extremely grateful. She proceeded to tell me some other issues regarding her family and that she had to start chemotherapy too. I reassured her and encouraged her not to be overwhelmed with everything that was happening but to take one step at a time.

I told her that God had sent me to her, that He had heard her cry and desperation for help. I had no idea what had just happened to her, but God sees and hears everything, and He sent help to her in her time of need.


Proverbs 15:3 (KJV)

*The eyes of the LORD are in every place, watching the evil and the good.*


The young woman listened to what I said as I proceeded to tell her everything that had happened to me earlier that day. Namely, putting the additional seats in the car, cleaning the car, the apology from one the member who would have taken the others home, being delayed after the meeting and then taking the other women home, all seemed to now make sense. Then seeing her on the street and hearing the voice say, Ask her if she is okay, nothing more and nothing less, and that was exactly what I did.

Had the evening not gone the way it did, I would have missed her and would not have seen her. I would not have been on the road at eleven o'clock that evening, but God saw her need at that time and He gave me the assignment to accomplish His task.

When we arrived at the station, she was met by the Police and she unloaded her suitcase, the pushchair and her baby. I could see the relief on her face that she now felt safe as they were going to find her a place of safety. As she left, she gave me a big hug and said, "You are an angel."

I said "No, God sent me to you as He saw your need."

She then said, "I think I am starting to believe." That warmed my heart as God had literally stepped into her world and provided her with the help that she needed.

When I returned home it was now midnight and I reflected on the events that had just happened. I sat down and was in awe of God. As previously said, I do not believe in coincidences, but I do believe in God's incidences. He had ordained and orchestrated everything that happened that evening from speaking to me to put the seats in the car, to me being delayed thus enabling me to be at that place where He showed me the young woman who was in distress. The following Sunday I shared the story with everyone at church and they too were blessed and touched by what had happened. The woman that was unable to attend the meeting due to being ill was also at church that Sunday morning and said, "I was sick for a reason," to which we both laughed. What a mighty God.

This testimony demonstrates what can happen when one comes into alignment with God and His word.


John 10:4 (KJV)

> ...and the sheep follow him: for they know his voice


I recognised that voice. It was not an audible loud voice but one that whispered in my heart. It comes with a peace and an assurance that God is with you so even though you do not know the outcome, you just know that everything will be okay. It is also a voice that gives you a choice. You choose your response and that response is usually coupled with trust and faith.

I also know that the Holy Spirit was speaking because I would not randomly think to approach a young woman late at night asking if she was okay. That was not in my thoughts as my thought was to get home so I could prepare for my friends coming the following day. No, God had an assignment for me that evening and that was to help the young woman and her child. God was also demonstrating His power by showing that He sees and knows all things. He demonstrated His power to me as His servant by directing me to help the young woman and he also demonstrated His power to the young woman by demonstrating a miracle at a time of desperation. We were both blessed by His intervention.

This testimony demonstrates that we are His hands and feet as my friend often says and He wants to show Himself to this world, through Christians who are willing to align themselves and be obedient to His word. This will then enable us to be assigned to whatever He wants us to do and therefore accomplish His will, which is for all mankind to know him.

John 3:16–17 (KJV)

> *For God so loved the world, that He gave His only begotten Son, that whosoever believeth in Him should not perish but have everlasting life.*
>
> *For God sent not His son into the world to condemn the world; but that the world through Him might be saved.*

I want to end with what was said at the beginning of this book.

John 10:10 (KJV)

> The thief cometh not, but for to steal, and to kill, and to destroy: I am come that they might have life, and that they might have it more abundantly.

John 10:10

> The thief's purpose is to steal, kill and destroy. My purpose is to give life in all its fullness.

God is Sovereign and He is still in control. We have the choice to align with Him so that He can demonstrate to people in this world that He is alive. Why not let him be the shepherd of your life today?

John 10:11 (KJV)

> I am the Good Shepherd: the good shepherd giveth his life for the sheep.

This highlights just how much we are loved. Metaphorically speaking, the good shepherd, Jesus Christ, gave His life for us, the sheep.

It is time to take back what the enemy has stolen and get back into alignment with God and His word so we can get on and be assigned to what He wants us to do and accomplish great things for Him. Only then can we live that abundant life promised to each and every one of us.

It is also important to state that coming into alignment, fulfilling our assignments and accomplishing great things for God is a journey and not a destination. Like living water, there should be a constant and refreshing flow that moves in our lives so that we, and others, can be impacted by God revealing Himself to us and to those around us. Do not allow fear, doubt or unbelief to cause a blockage in your life. These cause the *water* to become stagnant. Of course, this is easier said than done. We all face challenges and difficulties in our lives. If we make the decision that we want to become aligned and assigned in order to accomplish God's will, He will take us on that journey; not only take us, but lead us and guide us.

For those who are already Christians, imagine if we all fulfilled what God assigned for us to do; not only in our communities but also in our churches. The Bible talks about the Church being a part of the body of Christ.

1 Corinthians 12:27

*Now here is what I am trying to say: All of you together are the body of Christ, and each one of you is a separate and necessary part of it.*

We are all important to God; it does not matter how insignificant you perceive yourself to be. We are all important to Him, so much so that He even knows the number of hairs on our head.

Luke 12:7

*And He knows the number of hairs on your head. Never fear, you are more valuable to Him than a whole flock sparrows.*


God Bless You.

# Broken Identity

It all started when Adam and Eve gave in
Eve was deceived but Adam did sin.
The tempter successful with his cunning plan
From there came the curse upon earth and all man.
Our fellowship broken with Father,
Oh, how it broke His dear heart
Then came His plan of redemption, He knew from the start!

God knew man would disobey and go his own way
Seeking to establish his own wisdom to display
Look what I have accomplished! Come see what I've built!
Exalting himself and feeling no guilt
As time rolled on...man realised he was wrong
for turning from his Father,
The Alpha and Omega, the True and Holy one.

Our identity broken, shattered and scarred.
Who can help us now... we are permanently marred?
Jesus the Lamb, the Word dressed in flesh
Saw passed our faults and saw our needs instead.
Perfect Lamb, only He was found worthy
To restore all our hope and renew us to our former glory

Switching his place for the broken human race
Now we wear his righteousness,
as He seats us in heavenly places.

**H. Henry**

# Prayer

*Dear Jesus,*

*Thank you so much that you gave your life so that I can have an abundant life.*

*I truly desire to live my life in alignment with your will and to fulfil the plans and purposes you have for me.*

*I confess that I am truly sorry for the sins and offences I have committed towards you and I ask for your forgiveness.*

*I ask that you will be in the driving seat of my life and that you will lead me and guide me as I put my faith and trust in you from this day forward.*

*I choose to take a different direction in life. A direction that pleases you and honours you.*

*I know that I will be faced with challenges, but you said you would never leave me nor forsake me. (Deuteronomy 31:6)*

*Please help me and teach me through your Holy Spirit how to apply your Word, (The Bible) which is a manual to life as I embark on this journey with you.*

*Thank you Lord Jesus*

*Amen*

For further information the author can be contacted at **dsreynolds3as@gmail.com** or web address **www.poawm-uk.org**

# References

The King James Bible (KJV)

The Living Bible (TLB), copyright ©1971 by Tyndale House Foundation, Illinois.

The New International Version Bible (NIV), Copyright © 1973 1978 1984 2011 by Biblica, Inc.™

Gardner David E. (2003) The Trumpet Sounds for Britain, volumes 1, 2 and 3 in one edition.

Munroe, Dr Myles (2006) Kingdom Principles: Preparing for Kingdom Experience and Expansion.

**Websites**
https://www.oxfordlearnersdictionaries.com/definition/english/align
https://www.facebook.com/bureauofwisdom
https://writingexplained.org
https://www.davidpawson.org

www.ingramcontent.com/pod-product-compliance
Lightning Source LLC
Chambersburg PA
CBHW020033120526
44588CB00030B/252